W9-CDC-689

A Garland Series

The English Stage
Attack and Defense 1577 - 1730

A collection of 90 important works
reprinted in photo-facsimile in 50 volumes

edited by
Arthur Freeman
Boston University

A Second and Third Blast of Retrait from Plaies and Theaters

by

Anthony Munday

with a preface
for the Garland Edition by

Arthur Freeman

Garland Publishing, Inc., New York & London

1973

Copyright © 1973

by Garland Publishing, Inc.

All Rights Reserved

Library of Congress Cataloging in Publication Data

Salvianus, 5th cent.
    A second and third blast of retrait from plaies and
theaters.

    (The English stage: attack and defense 1577-1730)
    Facsimile reprint.
    Original t. p. reads: A second and third blast of
retrait from plaies and theaters: the one whereof was
sounded by a reuerend Byshop dead long since; the
other by a worshipful and zealous gentleman still alive;
one showing the filthines of plaies in times past; the
other the abhomination of theaters in the time present.
...Set forth by Anglo-phile Eutheo ...Allowed by
authority, 1580.
    "The second blast" is a translation of Book 6 of De
gubernatione Dei by Salvianus.
    "The first blast" is S. Gosson's The school of abuse.
    1. Theater--Moral and religious aspects.
I. Munday, Anthony, 1553-1633. II. Gosson, Stephen,
1554-1624. The school of abuse. III. Title.
IV. Series.
PN2051.S2 1973   792'.013   77-170405
ISBN 0-8240-0587-2

Printed in the United States of America

Preface

This self-declared sequel to Gosson's Schoole of Abuse *was entered to Henry Denham on 18 October 1580. The "Reuerend Byshop dead long since" is the fifth century presbyter of Marseilles, Salvianus, and to him belongs the "second blast" (* De Gubernatione Dei, *bk. vi.); the "worshipful and zealous Gentleman now aliue" one may identify with the translator himself, "Anglo-phile Eutheo," who has in turn been identified conventionally with Anthony Munday, one of the most prolific hacks of the Elizabethan age, and as a playwright himself nominated by Francis Meres in 1598 "our best plotter." The attribution seems to originate with F.J. Fleay,* A Chronicle History of the London Stage *(1890), p. 51, and has been followed with some caution by most scholars to the present.*

*William Ringler (*Stephen Gosson *[Princeton, N.J., 1942]) discusses in some detail the relationship of* A Second and Third Blast *to Gosson's original, which "Anglo-phile Eutheo" terms "the first blast in my compt." A curious echo of the*

5

PREFACE

various blasts may be the entry in SR *of 10 November 1580 to Edward White: "A Ringing Retraite Courageously sounded, wherein Plaies and Players are fytlie Confounded," (Arber, II, 174), which sounds like a ballad, otherwise unrecorded.*

Our reprint is prepared from British Museum 641.a.40, collating A-H^8 I^7 with Henry Denham's device on the recto of I7; $I7^v$ is blank. This was George Steevens' copy, Lot 1427 in the sale of 1800, when it was combined with Gosson's Schoole of Abuse *and attributed to Gosson; Dr. Burney purchased the volume for £717s. 6d., and Thomas Park notes in his own Steevens sale catalog "For H.M." Hazlitt included* A Second and Third Blast *in his* English Drama and Stage *(1869), from which text Chambers takes his extract (*Elizabethan Stage, *IV, 208-212).* STC *21677; Lowe-Arnott-Robinson 255.*

January, 1973　　　　　　　　　　　　A.F.

A second and third blast
of retrait from plaies
and Theaters :

the one whereof was founded by a re-
uerend Byshop dead long since ;
the other by a worshipful and
zealous Gentleman
now aliue :
one showing the filthines of plaies in
times past ; the other the abhomination of
Theaters in the time present :
both expresly prouing that that Common-weale is
nigh vnto the cursse of God, where-
as either plaiers be made of, or
Theaters main-
tained.

Set forth by Anglo-phile Eutheo.

Ephef.5, verfe.15,16.
Take heede therefore that ye walke circumspectlie, not
as vnwise, but as wise, redeeming the time,
because the daies are euil.

Allowed by auctoritie.
1586.

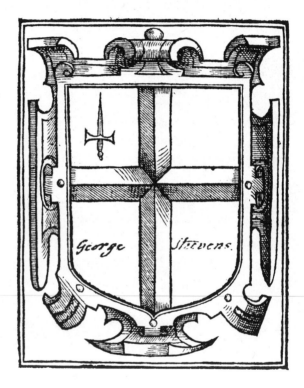

George Stevens.

Anglo-phile Eutheo to the Reader, S.

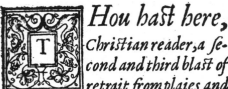

Hou haſt here, *Chriſtian reader, a ſe-* *cond and third blaſt of* *retrait from plaies and* *Theaters. The firſt blaſt in my compt* *is* The Schoole of abuſe: *a title not* *vnſitlie aſcribed vnto plaies. For* *what is there which is not abuſed* *thereby? Our hartes with idle cogita-* *tions; our eies with vaine aſpects,* *geſtures, and toies; our eares with* *filthie ſpeach, vnhoneſt mirth, and re-* *baldrie; our mouths with curſed ſpea-* *king; our heads with wicked imagi-* *nations; our whole bodies to vnclea-* *nes; our bodies and mindes to the* *ſeruice of the Diuel; our holie daies* *ith prophanes; our time with idle-*

Schoole
of abuſe.

nes;

M. Goſ-
ſon in his
inuectiue
againſt
plaies,cal
led The
Schoole
of abuſe.
b 3.Blaſt
of retrait
frō plaies.
c M.Spark
in his re-
herſal ſer-
mon at
Paules
croſſe,29.
of April.
Ann.1579.
d Clement.
Alexand.
li.3.Pædag.
cap.12.
e Cyril. Ca-
tech.1 .My-
ſtagogica.
f 2.blaſt of
retrait frō
plaies.
g Tertul.
lib. de ſpe-
ctaculis.

nes ; al our bleſſings, health, wealth,
and proſperitie to the increaſe of Sa-
tans kingdome, are there abuſed: that
not vnfitlie they are tèarmed, as of
late The ſchoole of abuſe, by one [a];
The ſchoole of Bauderie by another [b]; The neſt of the Diuel, and
ſinke of al ſinne, by a third [c], ſo long
agoe, The chaire of peſtilence, by
Clement Alexandrinus [d]; by Cyril [e],
and Saluianus [f] The pompe of the
Diuel; the ſoueraigne place of Satan, by Tertullian [g].

And albe I cal them, A ſecond and
third blaſt, &c. yet do I not ſo, as
though there were no moe blaſtes, or
dehortations frō them, or inuectiues
againſt them beſide . For in al ages
the moſt excellent men for learning
haue condemned them by the force of
eloquence, and power of Gods worde
(as I am to proue vpon anie good
occaſion offered). But ſo do I tearme
them

them *in respect of the time present wherein none, that I knowe, besides these Autors haue written, though manie, thanked be God, in the principal places of this land haue, and dailie, yea and openlie do speake against plaies and Theaters.*

Autor of ẏ second blaſt.

The former of these two was written in the Latine tong by that reuerend man Saluianus [h] *Bishop of* Maſsilia, *who for his wonderful eloquence and zeale is called,* Magiſter Epiſcoporum, *The maiſter of Byſhops, by* Gennadius [i]; *and that* 1100. *yeeres ſithence, VVherebie thou maiſt gather, firſt, that it is a moſt odious, & intolerable thing in a Chriſtian Common-weale, which ſo learned a Byſhop would ſtand to confute; & ſecondlie, that to dehort from plaies is no newe thing, being condemned ſo long ago.*

[h] Saluianus Maſſilienſis Epiſcopus lib. 6. de gubernat. Dei. [i] Gennadius de illuſtribus viris.

The Lord of his infinite mercie grant,

grant, that his blast maie do more good with Englishmen, than it did with the Romans, to which he founded the same. Otherwise I know right wel, that must needs betide vs which happened vnto them. For they contemned his saiengs, and the warnings of such like good men. Therfore first came the foraine enimies, the Gothes and Vandales who ouercame them, and oppressed them with most grieuous bondage; and afterward they fel into the handes of Satan, who caried them headlong into al impuritie of life, & abomination, vnder which curse of God they as yet continue. So we, assuredlie, vnles we listen vnto the dehortations of these good men, and shun plaies, with such like pompes of Satan, the which once we, when it was, before God & his congregation, renounced, shal fal into some one intolerable plague of

God

God or other, into the handes if not
of foraine enimies, which I feare; yet
of our spiritual aduersarie, the Pope
or Diuel, which I am sure of.

Touching the Autor of the latter
blast, thou maist coniecture who he
was, but I maie not name him at
this time for my promise sake: yet this
do I saie of him, that he hath bine, to
vse his verie wordes, A great affecter of that vaine Art of plaie making, &c. Yea, which I ad, as excellent an Autor of those vanities, as
who was best. But the Lord of his
goodnes hath called him home; so
that he did not so much delight in
plaies in times past, but he doth as
much detest them now, and is harti-
lie sorie that euer he was such an in-
strument to set vice afloate: as more
at large in his discourse, thou maist
perceaue. VVhereby first, note with
me, the goodnes of our God toward
vs,

vs, who *seeing that we wil not shun*
plaies for anie dehortations of his
godlie Preachers, who daie by daie
in al places of greatest resort de-
nounce the vengeance of GOD to
them, be they hie or lowe, that fauor
plaies, Theaters, or plaiers, stirreth
vp the verie Autors themselues to
inueigh against them, that we maie
be ashamed any waie to allowe that,
which the verie Autors do vtterlie
condemne . Secondlie praise God, I
beseech you, for bringing this Autor,
and Maister Gosson, *who made the*
Schoole of abuse out of Babylon. And
thirdlie praie vnto him, that al ma-
kers of plaies maie folowe their ex-
ample : then sure I am, that both the
rude multitude, if not for feare of
Gods displeasure, yet because they can
heare nothing but what is stale, wil
leaue haunting of stinking plaies;
and also plaiers themselues forsake
their

their vnlawful, vngodlie, and abominable exercise, for lacke either of Autors, or of auditors.

Loth was the Autor, I must needs confesse, to haue his worke published, not because he would not haue plaies openlie reproued, which from his hart he wisheth were most straightlie forbidden, but through a too too base conceipt of his owne worke, thinking that some grounded Diuine were more fit to dehort from so prophane an exercise, than he, whose profession (if so I maie saie) is otherwise. But hearing partlie by me, and partlie by others, what a ioie to the children of God, and griefe to the seruants of Satan it would be to heare, that he, who was so famous an Autor, was now become a religious dehorter from plaies; yea, thinking how the one sort would with more zeale auoide them, & the other with more shame

appeare

*appeare on stage, when they should
vnderstand that al the world know-
eth that their exercise is neither
warranted by Gods worde, nor liked
of Christians, but disalowed vtterly
by Scripture, by reason, by Doctors,
by Byshops, by their verie Autors
themselues, yea and by al other good
men, as the enimie to godlines, and
the corruption of the wel disposed,
and so consequentlie a special engine
both to subuert al Religion, and to
ouerthrowe the good state of that
Common-weale where it is maintained, he altered his minde, and
gaue me his booke, wishing me to do
therewithal as I thought best for the
glorie of God, and thy commoditie.*

*VVhich I haue now, together with
the inuectiue of that reuerend Bishop* Saluianus, *published, that one
of them might showe the abomination of Theaters in the time present,*
and

TO THE READER.

and the other how odious they haue
seemed to the godlie in time past,
and both allure thee vtterlie to forbid them, if thou be a Magistrate of
power, and to auoide them more
than anie pestilence, be thou
whosoeuer. VVhich
God grant.

A second blast of retrait
from plaies and Theaters,
sounded by that reuerend, god-
lie, and learned Byshop *Saluianus,*
sometime Byshop of Massilia, *in his*
sixt booke *De guber-*
natione Dei.

Vch thinges are
committed at plaies
and Theaters, as can-
not be thought vp-
on, much lesse vttered without
sinne. For other vices chalenge
their seueral portions within vs,
as filthie cogitations the minde;
vnchaste aspects the eies; wicked
speech the eares: so that when one
of these doth offend, the rest may
be without fault. But at Theaters
none of these but sinneth, for both
the mind there with lust; and the
eies with showes; and the eares
with hearing be polluted: al which
are so bad, that no man can wel

report

report or declare them with honeſtie.

For who, without paſſing the
boundes of ſhamefaſtnes, can vtter thoſe imitations of vnhoneſt
things ; that filthie ſpeech ; that
vile motion , the beaſtlie geſtures,
vſed there ? The vilenes whereof
may be gathered euen by the vn-
lawfulnes to name them. For ſom
ſinnes, though moſt hainous, may
wel and honeſtlie both be named,
& blamed too, as murder, theft, adulterie, ſacriledge , and ſuch like :
onlie the filthines of Theaters are
ſuch as may not honeſtlie be no
not ſo much as blamed. Such new
matter ariſeth againſt the reproo-
uer for finding falt with this moſt
horrible filthines; that albeit he be
a moſt perfect honeſt man that
would ſpeake againſt it, yet can he
not ſo doe and keepe his honeſtie.
Againe,

Againe, al other euils pollute the
doers onlie, not the beholders, or
the hearers. For a man may heare
a blafphemer, and not be partaker
of his facriledge, inafmuch as in
minde he diffenteth. And if one
come while a roberie is a doing, he
is cleere, becaufe he abhors the
fact. Onlie the filthines of plaies,
and fpectacles is fuch, as maketh
both the actors & beholders giltie
alike. For while they faie nought,
but gladlie looke on, they al by
fight and affent be actors, that trulie may be applied vnto them that
faieng of the apoftle, *How that not* Rom.1.31.
onlie they which commit fuch things
are worthie death, but alfo which fa-
uor them that do them.

So that in that reprefentation of
whoredome, al the people in mind
plaie the whores. And fuch as hap-
pilie came chafte vnto fhowes, returne

turne adulterers from plaies. For
they plaie the harlots, not then
onlie when they go awaie, but also when they come. For as soone
as one lusteth after a filthie thing,
whiles he hasteneth to that which
is vncleane, he becometh vncleane.

Now this being so, behold I
praie you, what partes either al or
almost al *Romans*, doe plaie. And
yet, we doing thus, saie we are not
regarded of God; we saie GOD
hath forsaken vs, when in verie
deede we forsake God.

God cannot
fauor such
as haunt
plaies.

For, suppose we, that our Lord
wil respect vs, not deseruing his
fauor? let vs see if he can. Lo, infinite thousandes of Christians doe
dailie abide at the showes of vnseemelie things. Can God then fauor such kinde of persons? Can
God cast his gratious countenance
vpon such as rage in circles, and
plaie

plaie the harlots in Theaters ? Or
is this our meaning, and doe we
thinke it meete,that forfomuch as
God feeth vs in circles, and Theaters,that what things we fee,he beholdeth ; and what filthines we
looke on, he feeth it alfo for companie ? For one of thefe muft
needes be : for if he vouchfafe to
looke vpon vs,it foloweth,that he
muft beholde al thofe thinges,
where we are : or if, which is moft
true, he turne awaie his eies from
thofe thinges, he muft likewife
turne his countenance frō vs who
are there. And the cafe ftanding
thus,yet naie-theles we doe thefe
things which I haue faid,and that
without ceffing.

Or thinke we that God hath his
Theaters , and circles , as had the
gods of the Gentils ? For thus did
they in old time , becaufe they
were

The Diuel delighteth in plaies; God detesteth them.

were perſuaded their idols deligh-ted in them. But how is it that we doe ſo, who are certaine that our God detesteth them? Or if wee knowe that this abominatiō doth pleaſe God, I wil not gaine-ſaie, but wee maie frequent it daie by daie. But if it be in our conſcience, that God abhorreth, that he dete-ſteth, that God is offended as the Diuel is fed by Theaters; how ſaie we that wee worſhip God in his Church, which ſerue the Diuel al-waies at plaies, and that wittinglie, and willinglie? And what hope ſhal we haue with God, who not ignorantlie, or by chance wound him, but after the example of thoſe gigants whome we reade, ful madlie bent themſelues againſt God, and againſt the cloudes. So we through the iniuries which al the world ouer continualie we in-fer,

fer, doe beate the heauens, as it were, with a common consent.

To Christ therfore, O monsterous madnes! euen to Christ doe we offer plaies and tomblers; yea and that especialie then when we receiue goodnes at his hands, whē we enioie prosperitie through his blessing, or God hath giuen vs victorie ouer the enimies, whereby what else do we show our selues, but euen iniurious to him which hath done vs good; to raile vpon him, who blesseth vs; to strike him ouer the face with a sworde, who louinglie doth kisse vs.

For I aske the mightie and rich men of this world, of what offence is that seruant guiltie, which wisheth il to a good and gratious maister, which raileth on him that deserueth wel; and rendereth despiteful wordes for benefits recei-

B.ij.　　ued?

ued? without controuersie al men
wil iudge him a most hainous offender, which for good rendreth il
to him, to whom indeed he might
not yeeld il for euil : euen thus do
we, which are called Christians;
we stir vp against vs a merciful
God by our vncleannes; we strike
a gratious God by our filthines;
we wound a louing God by our
wickednes.

To Christ therefore, ô monsterous madnes! euen to Christ doe
we offer plaiers and tomblers ; to
Christ we do render for his benefites the filthines of theaters; euen
to Christ do we sacrifice the obla-
tions of most beastlie sport. As
though our Sauior, who for vs became man, taught vs to doe so, and
had preached the same either by
himselfe, or by his Apostles ; as
though that to this end he tooke
                                    vpon

vpon him the fhame of mans na-
tiuitie, and the contumelious be-
ginnings of an earthlie generati- Luk.2, 12.
on; to that end he laie in a cratch, 13.
at what time notwithftanding
the verie Angels miniftred vnto
him ; to that ende he would be
fwadled with rags of cloth, who
gouerned the heauens in fimple
cloth ; to that end he hong on the
croffe, at whofe hanging the verie
world was aftonifhed. *VVho being* 2.Cor.8,9.
rich, faith the Apoftle, *for your fakes*
became poore, that yee thorough his
pouertie might be made rich. And Phil.2, 6.
being in the forme of G O D, he hum-
bled himfelfe vnto the death, euen
the death of the croffe : Euen this
did Chrift teach vs when he fuffered thefe things for our fakes.

Wel do we requite his paffion,
who, receiuing through his death
redemption, leade a moft filthie
life.

11. life. *For the grace of God that brin-*
geth saluation vnto al men hath ap-
12. *peared,* faith bleſſed Paule, *and*
teacheth vs that wee should denie
vngodlines, and worldlie luſtes, and
that wee should liue soberlie, and
righteouslie, and godlie in this pre-
13. *sent world, looking for the bleſſed*
hope, and appearing of the glorie of
14. *the mightie God, and of our Sauior*
Ieſus Chriſt, who gaue himselfe for
vs, that he might redeeme vs from
al iniquitie, and purge vs a peculiar
people vnto himselfe, zealous of good
workes.

    Where be they which doe theſe
things, for which the Apoſtle ſaith
Chriſt came? where be they which
flie the deſires of this world? where
be they which liue godlie & righ-
teouſlie, that looke for the bleſſed
hope by wel doing, and leading a
pure life, ſhow thereby that they
looke

looke and long for the kingdome of God; where be fuch?

Our Lord Iefus Chrift came, faith he,*that he might purge vs a peculiar people vnto himfelfe, zealous of good workes.* Where is that pure people? that peculiar people ; that good people, that people of holines?

Chrift, faith the Scripture, *fuffered for vs, leauing vs an enfample, that we should folow his fteps.* And we folow the fteps of our Sauior in circles, and in Theaters, we folow the fteps of our Sauior: as though our Sauior left vs fuch an enfample, whome wee read did weepe, but that he laughed, we neuer read. And both thefe for our fakes, becaufe weeping is a pricking of the hart, laughter the corruption of maners. Therefore faid he, *VVoe to you that laugh, for yee shal waile and weepe:* and, *Bleffed are*

are ye that weepe now, for yee shal
laugh. But it is not enough for vs
to laugh and be merrie, vnles we
reioice with fin and madnes; vnles our laughter be tempered with
filthines, & mixed with impietie.

What error, I faie, is this, naie
what foolifhnes? Can we not dailie be merrie, and laugh, vnles we
make our laughter & mirth to be
wickednes? Or els thinke we fimple mirth to be nothing worth?
and can wee not laugh except wee
finne? what a mifchiefe is this, naie
what furie? Let vs laugh, I praie
you, yea vnmeafurablie, and let vs
be merrie, yea continualie, fo we
finne not. What foolifhnes, naie
madnes is it, to thinke mirth and
ioie nothing worth, vnles God be
iniuried therebie? yea iniuried, &
that moft hainouflie?

For in fhowes there is a certaine
Apo-

Apostasie from the faith ; and a
deadlie declining from our beliefe,
and the heauenlie sacraments. For
what is the first professiõ of Christians at their baptisme? They pro-
test they wil renounce the Diuel,
and al his workes, his pompes, and
vanities. Therefore by our owne
confession, showes & pompes are
the workes of the Diuel.

To see plaies a kind of A-postasie.

How then, ô Christian, dost
thou haunt plaies and Theaters after baptisme, which thy selfe con-
fessest are the works of the Diuel!
Once thou didst renounce the Diuel and al his showes, wherebie it
foloweth, that whiles thou goest
witting and willinglie vnto common spectacles, thou must thinke
thou returnest again vnto the Diuel. For thou hast renoûced both,
and didst confesse one of them to
be both. So that returning vnto
one,

one, thou wenteſt back vnto both.
For, thou ſaieſt, I renounce the
Diuel, his pompes, ſhowes, and
workes. And what afterward ? I
beleeue, thou ſaieſt, in God the
Father almightie, and in Ieſus
Chriſt his ſonne. Therefore before
we can beleeue in God, the Diuel
muſt be renounced. For he belee-
ueth not in God, who renoun-
ceth not the Diuel. So then he for-
ſaketh God, who returnes to the
Diuel. But the Diuel is in his
pompes & ſhowes, then it foloweth that by returning vnto his
pompes wee forſake the faith of
Chriſt. Then hereby al the myſte-
ries of the Beliefe are vnloſed; and
al which foloweth in the Creede,
is weakened, and tottereth. For
the building cannot ſtand, if the
principal be downe.

Then tel me, ô Chriſtian, how
canſt

canſt thou think thy ſelfe to keepe
that which folowes in the Creed,
when thou haſt loſt the beginning
of the ſame? The members without an head be nothing worth; &
to their beginning al things haue
reſpect; which once being decaied
euerie thing goes to wracke. For
the roote being gone, either nothing remaines; or if there do, it
ſerues to ſmal profit, for without
an head nothing can ſtand.

He therefore that thinkes it a
light offence to ſee plaies, let him
conſider al what we haue ſaid, and
he ſhal ſee that in plaies there is
deſtruction, and no pleaſure. And
what els is it, but to fal into deſtruction, to forgo the beginning
of life? For where the fundacion
of the Beliefe is ouerthrown, life it
ſelfe is deſtroied.

Then againe we muſt needs returne

turne vnto that which we haue
often said: what such thing a-
mong the barbarous? where be a-
nie stages among them, or Theaters? where is the sinne of manie
sinnes, that is the destruction of

*Pagans
might bet-
ter erect &
frequent
Theaters
than Chri-
stians.*
our hope, and saluation? which
notwithstāding if they, being Pagans did vse, they should erre with
lesse offence of God: because albe
such doing were a defiling of the
sight, yet were it not a breaking of
the sacrament.

But now, what can we saie for
our selues? we hold the beleefe, &
we ouerthrowe the beleefe; wee
confesse the dutie of saluation, and
also denie the same. And therefore
where is our Christianitie? who,
as it seemeth, hereunto are baptized, that afterward more hainous-
ly we might offend? we prefer pastimes before the Church; we de-
spise

spife the Lordes table, and honor
Theaters; at a worde, we loue al
things, reuerence al things, God
alone feemeth vile to vs in com-
parifon of other things.

Finalie among the reft which
proue the fame, this which I now
faie, doth fhowe it to be true. For if
it fal out, as often it doth, that at
one & the fame time an holie daie
be kept, and common plaies procla-
med, I demaund, whether do men
flock moft, to the court of God, or
to the den of plaies; to the temple,
or to Theaters? And what do men
heare moft willinglie, the faiengs
of the Euangelifts, or the toies of
plaiers; the wordes of life, or the
wordes of death; the wordes of
Chrift, or the words of a foole in a
plaie? doubtles we loue that beft,
which we prefer. For if the Church
keepe anie feaft on that daie when
deadlie

deadlie paſtime is ſhowen, men,
ſuch as ſay they are Chriſtians, either come not at al vnto Church;
or, if not thinking of plaies they
come and heare in the ſame plaies
to bee abroad, they leaue the
Cuhrch. The temple is deſpiſed, to
run vnto Theatres; the Church is
emptied, the yeard is filled; wee
leaue the ſacrament, to feede our
adulterous eies with the impure, &
whoriſh ſight of moſt filthie paſtime. But forſooth we, whom proſperitie doth mar, muſt do ſome-
thing in the beginning. And therfore ful rightlie ſaith the Lord
God vnto vs; *For your vncleannes
are yee with deſtruction abolished.*
And againe, *The altars of this mirth
shalbe rooted out.*

But now it maie be anſwered,
that in al the townes of the *Romans* plaies be not vſed. True it is,
and

and I ad moreouer, that neither be
Theaters where in times paſt they
were. For they are not vſed neither at *Magontia,* nor at *Maſſilia,*
becauſe thoſe townes be ouerthrowen, and deſtroied; They are
not vſed at *Agrippina,* for the enimie hath ſubdued the ſame; not
in *Treuers* that famous towne, becauſe being foure-times ſubdued,
it is now brought to ground; to
conclude they are not vſed in moſt
townes both of *France,* and *Spaine;*
and therefore wo to vs men, and to
our vncleannes; wo to vs, and to
our wickednes. What hope is there
for Chriſtian people before God?
inaſmuch as thoſe euils haue neuer ben in *Roman* cities, ſince they
came into the hands of *Barbarians.*
Wherby it appeareth that wicked-
nes and impuritie, is proper & pe- *Romans*
culiar vnto the *Romans,* and their *ſingular*
wicked.
                verie

verie nature as it were. For there wickednes doth chieflie raigne, where the *Romans* be.

But haplie this maie seeme a grieuous, and vniust complaint: grieuous indeede, if it be false. But how, thou wilt saie, how can it be otherwise, sithence what we haue said, are done in a few cities of the *Romans*? And most of them are not polluted with this spot of filthines, where although the place and dwelling of ancient error do abide, yet are not those things now done which were in times passed.

It wil be good therefore to consider both these things, that is, both why the places & houses of plaies are yet vp; and yet no plaies vsed. The places and houses of filthines are therefore yet standing, because in them all impure things were wont to be showen: and now the

vaine

vaine paſtime is not vſed, for that the miſerie of the time, and mens pouertie will not permit. So that it was of their impietie, why in time paſt plaies were frequented, & neceſsitie is the cauſe that they are not now. For the miſerable caſe of the exchequer, & the emptines of the *Romane* treaſurie wil ſuffer no monie to be waſted commonlie vpō trifling things. And although much is loſt, and caſt as it were vpon the dunghil: yet nothing ſo much can be conſumed, becauſe they haue not wherewithal to do ſo. For ſuch is our inſatiable deſire of filthie pleſure, that we could wiſh to haue more, onlie to laie it vpon this dirte of abhomination. And the thing ſhowes what we would prodigalie conſume, if we were rich, when we waſt ſo much being in ſo poore a ſtate. For this

C.j.　　　is

is the ſpot, and miſerie of the preſent time, that although through
pouertie we cannot, yet through
our impietie we would conſume
much.

There is no cauſe then why we
ſhould deceaue our ſelues, in ſaieng that in al cities thoſe things
are not, which were before done.
For therefore they are not in this
time vſed, becauſe the townes
where they were vſed, are not to
be ſeene: and where they haue a
long time bene vſed, there is not
to bring it to paſſe: as God himſelfe ſpeaketh vnto ſinners by the
prophet, *And it aſcended vpon his*
harte, and the Lord could beare it
no longer: for the wickednes of
your ſtudies, and for the abhomina-
tions which you haue committed,
and your land is brought into de-
ſolation, into barrennes, and accur-
ſed.

sed. This is the caufe then whie the maior part of the *Romane* empire is brought into defolation, into barrennes, and accurfed.

And would to God they were onlie done in times paft, and not now in thefe daies, happelie then, as it is written, God would be merciful to our finnes. But we take not the waie to haue Gods fauor. For vnceffantlie we ad finne to fin, & heape wickednes vpon wickednes, that as the better part of vs are deftroied, fo we maie al come to nought.

For, I demand, who feeth another flaine before his face, and is not afraide? who beholdeth his neighbors houfe on fire, and wil not by al meanes prouide for the falfetie of his owne? wee do not onlie fee our neighbors to burne, but alfo are fet on fire our felues

from the chiefeſt part of our bodies. And, ô abomination! what a
miſchiefe is this? we burne, we
burne, yet dread we not the fire
wherwith we burne. For, as I ſaid,
the cauſe why thoſe things which
before time were vſed, are not
now done, is to be aſcribed to the
miſerie we are in, not to anie diſ-
cipline or good order which we
haue.

Finalie, I doe eaſilie prooue the
ſame. For make the time as it was,
and forthwith al things ſhalbe as
they were in thoſe daies. Yea
moreouer, as touching the deſire
of men, though thoſe things are
not euerie where, yet in reſpect of
their minds euerie where they be.
For the *Romans* would haue them
vſed euerie where. For when neceſsitie onlie makes an euil thing
to be left vndone, the verie deſire

of

of a filthie thing is condemned in such fort as if it were done. For, as I faie, according to the wordes of our Sauior, *VVhofoeuer looketh on* Matt.5, 28. *a woman to luſt after her, hath cõmitted adulterie with her alreadie in his harte :* whereby we maie gather, that albe we leaue things filthie & damnable vndone, and that onelie through necefsitie; yet becaufe our wil is good to haue them, wee are guiltie of condemnation.

And what fpeake I of wil? when almoſt euerie where thofe things are committed. For what ſtranger foeuer commeth either to *Rauenna,* or to *Rome,* ſhal finde a part of the *Romans* at fhowes; and a part of the *Rauenians* at Theaters. And although anie be either abfent, or diſtant by place, yet is he not excufed thereby. For as manie

as

as are ioined togither in likenes of
affection, are guiltie alike of the
fame wickednes which either do
commit.

Yet for al this wee flatter our
felues of our good behauior; wee
flatter our felues of the rarenes of
impuritie. But I fay yet more, that
not onelie thofe foule fpots of infamous plaies are yet to be feene
as afore time; but alfo be more a-
bominablie fet forth, than euer
they were. For in thofe daies euerie part of the *Romane* empire was
in health and found; the riches of
other townes made the common
barnes to be large & big; citizens
did abound in wealth and pleafure, fo that it was verie hard in
fuch aboundance of al things, for
religion to continue pure, and
manners vncorrupt. Then euerie
where Autors of filthie pleafure
                              were

were cherished; for in al places men were fat. No man waide the charge of the Common-weale, no man feared to come behind hand; for expenses was not perceaued. The Common-weale after a sort did seeke where, and how to wast wealth, hauing almost no place to keepe it. And therefore heapes of wealth, euen wel nigh aboue measure, were consumed vpon vaine things.

But now what maie be said? old aboundance is gone, gone is the wealth which once we had. Poore wee are, yet cease wee not to be vaine. And whereas pouertie doth reclaime prodigal and prodigious pupils, so that when their wealth is gone, they leaue wickednes: we showe our selues a newe kind of pupils and vnthriftes, who lacking wealth wil not leaue wickednes.

Whereby

Whereby it appeareth, that the cause of our wickednes, is not in the inticements, as of other men, but in our hartes : and that our mindes, is our wickednes; that in deede not by the taking awaie of riches, but through the desire of euil things we sinne.

And although we haue hither-to recited manie vices of the *Romans*, which the barbarous people are not polluted withal : yet are there manie mo, which I wil now ad. But first this I warne you by the waie, that you account no kind of sinne light, which tendeth vnto the dishonor of God. For if no man maie dishonor him that is noble and mightie; but if he do so he is made to answere it where he would not, and condemned by lawe : how much more hainous is that offence, whereby the glorie

of

of God is defaced? For alwaies the fault doth increase, according to the worthines of him that is iniuried. Because by how much the person is greater that suffereth reproch, by so much is he faultie that doth the same. Whereof it is which wee read in the lawe, that they which to mans thinking did but lightlie offend, were most seuerelie for al that punished: which was to giue vs to vnderstand that nothing, which concerneth God, should be lightlie accounted of: & that that which man esteemed a smal offence, because it was committed against the glorie of God, was a most grieuous crime.

To be short, *Vzza* that Leuite of the Lord, what did he contrarie vnto the commandement of God, when he assaied to keepe vp the Arke of God from falling? no precept

Exod. 31, verse. 13. 14

*Nomb.*20, verse. 25. 26,&c.

*Nomb.*25, verse. 4. 9.

1.Chr. 13, verse. 9. 10.

Vzza.

cept was there by lawe to forbid him ; yet while he held vp the same, presently through the wrath of God he died : not becaufe he had done anie thing rebelliouſlie, or at leaſtwiſe not dutifullie, but by ſhowing dutie he prooued vn-dutiful, for taking more vpon him than he was commanded.

Gathering of ſtickes. *Nomb.15, verſe. 32. 35. 36.* That man among the people of Iſrael, that had gathered ſtickes vpon the Sabboth daie, died the death, and that by the iudgement, and commandement of God, euen the moſt gratious and mercifull iudge, who out of doubt had ra-ther pardon than kil, had not the conſideration of ſeueritie preuai-led ouer his mercie. For one raſh felowe periſhed, that manie after-ward through raſhnes might not periſh.

And what ſhould I ſpeake of each

each particular man? The whole Nomb.11,
nation of the Iewes traueling tho- verse. 4.
rough the wildernes, becaufe they 31.
lufted after their wonted meate, 32.
loft a part of their people. Yet was Pfa.78,30.
there no cōmandement that they 31.
fhould not luft, but God, as I fup-
pofe, would prouide afore hand
for the due obferuation of the
moral law, by reftraining their re-
bellious concupifcence: euen that
al the people might the more eafilie confeffe, how earneftlie they
fhould auoid thofe things, which
God in his holie Scripture fhould
forbid, when they were punifhed
for that, which as yet they were
not forbidden.

The fame people alfo complai-
ned that they tooke fuch paines,
for which caufe the Lord plagued
them from heauen: not becaufe a
man oppreffed with labor might
not

not complaine; but for that therebie they showed themselues vn-
thankful towards G O D, making
God, as it were, the Autor of their
immoderate busines. Wherby we
maie gather, how zelouslie hee
ought to serue God, which enioi-
eth prosperitie, when as he maie
not complaine being in aduersitie.

But perchance, some wil saie,
whereto serues al this? whether
to? doubtles, that we should count
nothing a smal thing, which hur-
teth the glorie of God. We speake
of common plaies, the verie mockerie of religion, and the toies of
our life. For while wee plaie at
Theaters and stages, we are rauish-
ed with the loue therof, according
to that in the holie Scripture, *It is
a pastime for a foole to do wickedlie.*
And so, in laughing at filthie and
abhominable thinges, we commit
wicked-

*Plaies the
mockerie of
religion.*

Prou. 10,
verse. 23.

wickednes : & thofe: no fmal fins,
but therefore the more damnable :
becaufe though they feeme fmal
at the firft fight, yet are they moft
peftilent in the end. For inafmuch
as there be two moft notorious e-
uils, as when a man either flaieth
himfelfe, or defacet]h the glorie of
God, both they are done in common plaies. For at plaies both the
euerlafting faluation of Chriftian
people is quite extinguifhed tho-
rough wicked filthines, & the maieftie of God violated, through fa-
crilegious fuperftition . For it is
certaine that it offendeth God, being confecrated to idols.

Two moft notorious offences cõmitted by frequenting plaies.

For *Minerua* in fchooles of exercife, *Venus* at Theaters, *Neptune*
at circles, in the field *Mars, Mercu-
rie* at wreftling places is adored, &
had in honor: and fo, according to
the qualitie of the Autors, fuperftition

ſtition doth encreaſe.

Al vncleanes is ſhowed at plaieng; al luxuriouſnes at wreſtling;
at tumbling al vnſhamefaſtnes;
al madnes in caues. Vncleannes is
one where; wantonnes anotherwhere, anotherwhere intemperan-
cie, and madnes anotherwhere: but
the Diuel is eueriewhere; yea in e-
uerie particular place where plaies
be, are al the ſortes of Diuels. For
they gouerne thoſe places which
are dedicated vnto them . And
therefore the onelie inticement is
not there, nor wickednes onelie in
ſuch ſpectacles, or ſhowes. For it
is a kind of ſacriledge beſide for a
Chriſtian to be at ſuch ſuperſtiti-
on; becauſe he taketh part with
their idolatrie, whoſe feaſts he is
delighted withal.

The which albeit alwaies it hath
bene a lamentable thing: yet then
is

is it moſt intollerable, when as be-
ſides the cuſtomable vſe of life, either our aduerſitie, or proſperitie
doth make it the more hainous.
And that becauſe God in aduerſitie ſhould be the more pacified, &
leſſe offended in proſperitie. For
Gods fauor ſhould be ſought for
when he is angrie; and when he is
mereiful, he ſhould not be diſho-
nored . For we fall into aduerſitie
through the diſpleaſure of God;
and by his fauor, we enioie proſperitie.

But we doe al things cleane o- *Proſperitie*
therwiſe. How ſo? doe you aske? *abuſed.*
marke what I ſaie. And firſt when
God being intreated of his owne
mercie (for wee do neuer ſo liue,
that we can deſerue to haue him
entreated) but, as I ſaie, when God
hath entreated himſelfe, and giuen
vs a peaceable time, great encreaſe,

2

a rich tranquillitie, and ſtore of al
thinges more than we can deſire;
then we ſo corrupt our ſelues with
ſuch proſperitie, and ſo defile our
liues with wickednes, that we vtterlie forget both G O D and our
ſelues. And whereas the Apoſtle
ı.Tim. 2, ſaith, that *The frute of peace which*
verſe. 2. *God doth ſend, conſiſteth in this, that*
we ſhould lead a peaceable and quiet
life in al godlines, and honeſtie : we
vſe the ſame as though God gaue
it to the end, that we ſhould liue
in al drõkennes, in al riotouſnes, in
naughtines, in theft, and in al wickednes and diſhoneſtie: as though
the benefite of peace giuen, were
leaſure to do wickedlie; and wee
ſhould take the truce of tranquillitie at Gods hand the more licen-
tiouſlie, and ſecurelie to ſinne.

Therefore wee are vnworthie
Gods gifts, which vſe the benefits
of

of God so wickedly. We make the occasion of good workes , to be onlie the matter of wickednes. Wherebie commeth to passe, that peace it selfe is against vs . For so we deale, that better it were for vs to be without that thing whereby we proue the worse.

Who would thinke it? we change the course of things by our wickednes; and what God of his mercie made good, we make the same il for vs, through our vile behauior, &c.

It remaineth that we now proue that neither the giftes nor alluremets of God do better vs one iote. And what are they? what, but euen our peace, quietnes, & tranquillitie which we enioie according to our wish and desire. Wherfore because the matter doth so require, let vs vtter some special thing.

Then, as often as we are in feare,
in affliction, in perils; when either
cities with enimies are befieged,
or countries by inuafion or anie
other aduerfitie are wafted . then
we beate the members of a Common-weale, and by praier cal for
the afsiftance of God . If by the
aide of God either townes be fa-
ued, or fpoile and pilling hath an
end; or the hoft of enimies foiled;
& al feare through the blefsing of
God is taken awaie , what do wee
ftraight after al thefe things? I beleeue we endeuor to requite the
benefits that we haue receiued frõ
our Lord God with feruing, ho-
noring, and reuerencing his holie
Name.(For this followeth,& ex-
perience doth prooue , that they
who are thankeful, get moe benefits, and they are bleffed with moft
ample and frefh rewardes that requite

Ironia.

quite good turnes.)

So happelie we do,& requiting our G O D at. leaftwife after the máner of men,we render good for his benefites, that is, we forthwith make recourfe vnto the houfe of the Lord; throwe out felues vpon the ground; praie vnto him. with ioie and teares together; fet forth the temple with our gifts, and be-ftowe rewards. And becaufe tho-rough his gift we are made merrie, we fhowe the fignes of our ioie in his téples, or at leaftwife,which he likes as wel, we renounce the for-mer wickednes of our life; flaie the facrifices of good workes; and for newe confolations we offer the fa-crifice of a new conuerfation; fina-lie we proclame an holie warre a-gainft al vncleannes ; fhun the madnes of ftages ; abhor the filthi-nes of plaies; promife a new life to the Lord, and finalie for the attainement of his perpetual protection we offer vp our selues wholie vnto God.

Now, forasmuch as these things which we haue metioned, should be done for Gods benefites newlie extended vpon vs, let vs consider what is done. Wee run forthwith vnto plaies, we flie vnto madnes, the people disperse themselues in Theaters, the whole multitude reuel it out at stages. He bestoweth good thinges vpon vs, that wee should be good; we contrariewise when we haue receaued good, encrease our wickednes; He by his benefites calleth vs vnto godlines, we therby fal to sin; He by his gifts allureth to repentace, we rush vnto vncleannes; He calleth vnto puritie of life, we folowe filthines.

Thus we wel requite him for his libe-

liberalitie , we do wel either ac-
knowledge, or honor him for his
giftes, who as greatlie do recom-
penſe him with iniuries,as he
hath mercifullie bleſt vs
with benefits.

FINIS.

A third blaſt of retrait
from plaies and Theaters,
showing the abhomination
of them in the time preſent.

 Nowlege makes
her ſeate & abode in
the mindes of thoſe
men,who are neither
addicted to their owne opinion ;
nor

nor yet carried awaie with euerie
likelihood of troth. For as he that
is vnwilling to heare, is furtheſt
from knowledge: ſo he that is carried awaie with euerie likelihood,
before he haue waded far & deep-
lie in the cauſe, ſhal prooue but
ſlender of iudgement. But he who
neuer wil be ſatiſfied with reaſon
maie rightlie be counted obſtinate
and peruerſe; and without reaſon
to be perſuaded commeth either
of ſimplicitie, or compulſion.

I write this to none other end
but to ſhowe, that as I ought not,
being wedded too much to mine
owne opinion, to be caried to the
defence of a wrõg cauſe: ſo it doth
not beſeeme me ouerlightlie to be
miſled vnto error through the cenſure of thoſe, whoſe bare affir-
mation or denial ſerue onelie to
maintaine, but not to prooue; for
that

that men are not to be satisfied
with wordes, but with reason.
Which if I maie be, I wil not be
counted a peruerse wrangler, but
franklie wil condescend into the
opinion of the wise: otherwise am
I to be pardoned, though I stand
ernest & stiffe against that which
is contrarie to virtue ; disagreeing
from good religion ; furthest from
ciuilitie, and maie neither by ar-
gument of reason, nor power of
learning be defended.

Such doubtles is mine opinion
of common plaies, vsual iesting,
and riming ex tempore, that in a
Christian-weale they are not sufferable . My reason is, because
they are publike enimies to virtue, & religion ; allurements vnto
sinne; corrupters of good manners;
the cause of securitie and careles-
nes; meere brothel houses of Bauderie;

derie; and bring both the Gospel into slander; the Sabboth into contempt; mens soules into danger; and finalie the whole Commonweale into disorder.

Great and hainous speeches, no doubt: yet not so hainous, as the exercise of them is odious; biting wordes, yet not so bitter as the cause requireth.

It were il painting the Diuel like an Angel, he must be portraied forth as he is, that he maie the better be knowen. Sinne hath alwaies a faire cloake to couer his filthie bodie. And therefore he is to be turned out of his case into his naked skin, that his nastie filthie bodie, and stinking corruption being perceaued, he might come into the hatred and horror of men. For as we are naturalie of our selues euil and corrupt: so are we naturalie

giuen

giuen to loue our felues, and to be
blinded with our owne affe&ions,
infomuch that, what we knowe
to be euil, we are not afhamed either openlie to defend, or flilie to
cloake.

The excufe of wickednes is but
the increafe of punifhment; & an
il caufe defended by au&oritie, &
maintained by learning , bringes
Magiftrates into flander, and learning into contempt.

This I fpeake, for that I knowe
thofe afore-faid do want neither
countenance to vphold, nor yet
fkil to defend them. But yet, vnder
corre&ion, an euil caufe maintained is nearetheles euil; &, as pitch
defiles the toucher thereof, be he
neuer fo cleane: fo the virtuous
bring their life into queftion either by fufferáce, or maintenance
of euil. For who wil not iudge but
what

what a man allowes in another,
he commendes in himfelfe?

I therefore with reuerence, not
as a teacher, but as a wel-willer
both to the noble and learned,
would wifhe them with *Adrian*
the Emperor to fuffer no paftime,
that maie bring them to vanitie;
nor to frequent that recreation
which tendes either to the hurt of
a Common-weale, or to the ouerthrowe of religion.

It is true that one opinion maie
be contrarie to another; and that
for the difliking of one or two, the
qualitie of plaieng were not to be
laid off, being fo highlie efteemed
of al fortes of men, for that euerie
man conceaueth of the goodnes
or badnes of a thing according as it
feemeth in his owne opinio. And
therefore the thing which they
difcommend, maie be both liked,
and

and allowed.

I confeſſe the iudgement of one
or two is not to be allowed in ſuch
caſes : neuertheles the opinions of
the rude multitude are not alwais
the ſoundeſt, which are mooued
with vnconſtant motions, whereby manie-times they like of that
which is moſt hurtful; and diſlike
that which is moſt profitable : becauſe the one pleaſeth their humors, and the other reſtraineth
their affections. The cenſure therfore of them who carie beſt groũd
from Gods worde; and is moſt a-
greeable to reaſon, moſt profitable
for the Cõmon-weale; leaſt hurtful to our brethren; and tending
alonelie to the reformation of abuſe, is ſooneſt to be allowed, and
followed.

Then, whether this my iudgmẽt
be to be admitted or no, as being

ing the foundeft, & refpecting the
benefit of this our countrie, I leaue
it to the iudgement of the godlie
wife, and learned. And that I maie
feeme to write nothing without
ground, or to finde fault without
caufe, I wil, G O D to freend, fet
downe nothing to prooue mine
affertion good, but what Scripture
fhal warrant, examples confirme,
reafon allowe, and prefent experi-
ence ratifie.

Which mine arguments, if anie
by more colour of truth can ouerthrowe, I am readie to recant, and
to allowe that for good, which I
can yet but condemne as wicked,
and thinke of al other to be the
moft intolerable abufe in our Cōmon-weale. For otherwife I cannot thinke, vnles I be conftrained,
as *Petrarch* faith, to iudge by other
mens iudgements; which who fo
doth,

doth, iudgeth not of himfelfe, but reportes the opinion of others.

Manie run on their courfes ve- rie vainelie, til it pleafe God to cal them home by the Spirit of his grace vnto amendment of life. For when it fhal pleafe him to touch the confcience of the wicked with repentance, the whole ftate of their life doth alter from that it was be- fore : as maie appeare in S. Paule at his conuerfion. And affuredlie the Lord doth fuffer vs manie- times to run paft our felues, that when he hath called vs home, we maie become examples of virtue and godlines vnto others.

I confeffe that ere this I haue bene a great affecter of that vaine art of Plaie-making, infomuch that I haue thought no time fo wel beftowed, as when my wits were exercifed in the inuention of those

The Autors former ftu- die; and life.

those follies; I might scarselie with
patience heare anie man speake,
were he neuer so learned and godlie, that thought to persuade me
from them. So far was I from re-
ceauing of their good and godlie
admonitions, that I stopped mine
eares, and hardened mine harte a-
gainst their counsel. Such is our
peeuish nature; we can like of nothing which doth dislike vs, or seemeth contrarie to our vaine opinions. And therfore it is God onlie, that must turne our mindes, o-
therwise wee shal neuer discerne
profitable from hurtful things. For
albe we haue some about vs, who
counsel vs the best, and seeke our
profit: yet for al that our nature is
so peruerse & froward, that what
is wel said wil take no place. This
found I by my selfe, & this I now
perceaue to be in others: but the
Lordes

Lordes purpoſe is good in al his dealings.

It might haue bene ſaid of me then, as it was written of the wicked, that *They conſidered not the waies of the Lord,* but after when it pleaſed God of his mercie to cal mee to the reading of his worde, and diligent ſtudie of the Scriptures , I began to loath my former life, and to miſlike my owne doings ; and I was no ſooner drawen with an hartie deſire to returne vnto the Lorde, but I found my ſelfe ſtrengthened with his grace vnto good deſires. For the Lord neuer faileth them that ſeeke him. Aſſuredlie his promiſe can neuer deceaue men, but when they knock, the gate ſhalbe opened vnto them ; & when they ſeeke, they ſhal find. There is nothing

Hereby learne thou, good Reader, how to ſhun not onelie the vanitie of plaies, but al other vanities, after the example of the Autor, who by diligent reading the holie Scriptures, and repentance, fel into an vtter deteſtation of plaies.

Luke.11,9.

What God requireth at our hands. thing more required in vs, than a readie desire of wel doing, who no doubt, being trulie ingraffed in our minds, shalbe so watered with the dewe of Gods holie spirit, that it wil increase and growe vp in vs to a more ful grouth and perfection.

When I came to a streit examination of my life, which I had *Plaies cannot abide the truth of Gods word.* vainelie consumed in those exercises; and that I began to cal mine old doings into question, and to trie them by the true tuch of Gods word, I found what I counted for gold to be but drosse, vile, and of *Vaine plaies make vaine folkes.* none account, hauing the propertie to make their fauorers of their owne nature.

The ende why this booke was made. Then to the end that others should not be deceaued with that wherewith my selfe was ouertaken, I thought it my part to laie open to al mens eies the horrible

abuse

abuſe aſwel of plaies as of the In-
actors, & the diſorder of their Auditorie; that the abuſe being perceaued, euerie man might reforme
himſelfe, & be weaned from their
wickednes; or otherwiſe, that the
Magiſtrats being informed might
take ſuch good waies, that the intolerable exerciſe of plaies might
be vtterlie put downe. For I am
verilie perſuaded, that if they may
be permitted ſtil to make ſale of
ſinne, we ſhal pul on our heads
Gods vengeance, & to our realme
bring an vtter confuſion.

What I ſhal ſpeake of the abuſe
by plaies of my owne knowledge,
I know maie be affirmed by hun-
dreds, to whome thoſe matters are
as wel knowen as to my ſelfe.
Some citizens wiues, vpon whom *Frutes of*
the Lord for enſample to others *plaies for*
the Diuels
hath laide his hands, haue euen on *owne mouth*

E.j. their

their death beds with teares con-
feffed, that they haue receiued at
thofe fpectacles fuch filthie infe-
ctions, as haue turned their minds
from chaft cogitations, and made
them of honeft women light huf-
wiues; by them they haue difho-
nored the veffels of holines; and
brought their hufbandes into contempt, their children into queftiõ,
their bodies into ficknes, and their
foules to the ftate of euerlafting
damnation.

He that toucheth pitch wilbe defiled.

Such is the nature and inclination of vs al, that we run whether
affection leades vs, and are withdrawen by companie. And therefore, as Dauid faith, *VVith the godlie thou wilt showe thy selfe godlie
with the vpright man thou will
showe thy selfe vpright. VVith the
pure thou wilt shewe thy selfe pure
and with the froward, thou will
show*

1.Cor. 6,
verfe. 19.
20.

2.Sam. 22,
verfe. 26.
27.
Pfa.18, 25.
26.

The repaire of them that are ho- *Auoid su-*
nest to thofe places of euil refort, *fpected pla-*
makes their owne good life to be *ces.*
doubted of; for that the place
breedes fufpicion afwel of good,as
of bad. For who can fee man or
woman refort to an houfe which
is notorioullie wicked, but wil
iudge them to be of the crewe of
the wicked and vngodlie?

The moft honeft wife, is the *The beft*
fooneft affalted, and hath fuch *fooneft*
fnares laid to entrap her,as,if God *tempted.*
afsift her not, fhe muft needes be
taken.

When I gaue my felfe firft to
note the abufe of common plaies,
I found mine harte fore fmitten
with forowe (finne did there fo a- *Horrible*
bound & was fo openlie commit- *finnes open-*
ted, that I looked when God in *lie commit-*
iuftice would haue prefentlie in *ted at The-*
aters.

E.ij. his

his wrath haue cōfounded the be-

Marke this, ô yee fauorers, frequēters, & vpholders of plaies.

holders.) The Theater I found to be an appointed place of Bauderie; mine owne eares haue heard honeſt women allured with abhominable ſpeeches. Sometime I haue ſeene two knaues at once importunate vpon one light huſwife, whereby much quarel hath growen to the diſquieting of manie. There ſeruants, as it is manifeſtlie to be prooued, haue conſented to rob their maiſters, to ſupplie the want of their harlots; there is the practiſing with married wiues to traine them from their huſbands, and places appointed for meeting and conference.

Who can fauor plaies when the Autors thē. ſelues abhor them.

When I had taken a note of al theſe abuſes, & ſawe that the Theater was become a conſultorie houſe of Satan, I concluded with my ſelfe, neuer to imploie my pen

to

to fo vile a purpofe, nor to be an
inftrument of gathering the wicked togither.

It maie feeme I am ouer lauifh
of fpeech ; and that which I haue
publiquelie expreffed of others by
mine owne knowledge might haue
bene diffembled . But I haue learned that he who diffembles the e-
uil which he knowes in other
men, is as giltie before God of the
offence, as the offenders thefelues.
And the Lord hath expreflie com-
manded in *Exodus,* that *we should* Exod. 23,
not folowe a multitude to do euil, verfe. 2.
neither agree in a controuerfie to
decline after many, and ouerthrawe
the truth. I cannot therefore but
refift fuch wickednes, leaft I might
feeme to maintaine them. For he
that diffembles vngodlines is a
traitor to God.

Since therefore that the caufe is
Gods,

Gods, I dare preſſe forth my ſelfe
to be an Aduocate againſt Satan
vnto the rooting out of ſinne. For
I am fully reſolued in Gods truth,
to build ſo ſtrong and ſure a fun-
dation againſt theſe ſellers, & ſet-
ters forth of ſinne, as neither they,
nor their adherents ſhal euer be
able to ouerthrowe. And my truſt
is that the godlie wil ioine with
me to the ſuppreſsing of thoſe
which fight againſt his worde, wa-
ging their battel on the Sabboth
daie the more conuenientlie to de-
ſtroie the ſoules of the children of
God.

　　The cauſe is generalie to be defended, for that the contention of
the Aduerſaries is about religion,
and therefore none can be diſchar-
ged for bare ſaieng they conſent
not to the wicked. For it is the
part of euerie true ſoldier of Ieſus
Chriſt

Chrift with al power to with-
ftand,& refift fuch as offer wrong
to the maieftie of G O D,by hin-
dering the feruice which we owe
vnto him. We are to be enimies
vnto the death againft thofe vpholders of wickednes;and neuer to
giue ouer the battel in fo holie, &
iuft a quarel.

We fee the wicked are alwaies
readie to maintaine euil caufes, &
in thefe daies the worft men fhal
find bearers,and bolfterers, and be
fupported by thofe,who by iuftice
are to fuppreffe them,or at leaft to
reforme their abufes,which are intolerable. If the wicked lurke together to vphold their lewdenes,
how much more ought the faith-
ful to ioine themfelues together
to plucke downe vanitie!

I knowe my felfe a worme of
al other the weakeft to medle in
thefe

thefe cafes: yet fuch is my defire
to ouerthrowe their wickednes,
that I dare, inflamed with the holie zeale of *Dauid* in the quarel of
God, vnprouided both of armor
and weapon, with one poore fling
refift the ftrength of their hugeft
Champion, and endure the brunt
of his fierce affalts; doubting not
but to finde fome that wil ftande
with me to ouerthrowe the enimies of G O D, and to pul downe
thofe flags of defiáce, which Satan
hath fet vp againft the preaching
of the Gofpel to the decaie of the
Church.

Let vs delaie no time, deere brethren, their doings are abhominable in the fight and eares of God,
and condemned of the righteous:
if therefore fentence againft their
euil workes be not executed fpee-
delie, *The hartes of the children of*
men,

men, as Ecclesiastes saith, *wilbe ful-* Eccl.8, 11.
lie set in them to do euil.

If there were nothing to moue *Plaies do*
you, but the breach of Gods com- *not onelie*
hinder the
mandement, it were great cause to *Gospel, but*
stir vp your godlie furie, and zeale *hurte the*
Common-
to discommend plaies vtterlie: but *weale.*
their abuses stretching further into the Common-wealth, are by
sufferance growen so huge, that it
is hard dealing with them as a-
gainst foes; for they are become *Waies how*
priuate freends. They are therfore *to suppresse*
plaies.
to be delt withal by degrees. For
it is verie hard to roote out that
frō our hartes, be it neuer so great
an abuse, wherof we haue concea-
ued a good opinion.

Let therefore the Magistrate but *The Magi-*
repel them from the libertie of *strates du-*
tie in sup-
plaieng on the Sabboth daie. For *pressing*
plaies.
that is the abuse which is generalie found fault withal, & allowed
of

of none but thoſe who are altoge-
ther deſtitute of the feare of God,
and without conſcience. To plaie
on the Sabboth is but a priuiledge
of ſufferance, and might with eaſe
be repelled, were it throughlie folowed. The warrant which Magiſtrats haue to forbid plaies is great,
and paſſed vnto them by ſuch a
Prince, whoſe auctoritie is aboue
al auctories of earthlie gouernors.

Exo.20, 8.
9.
10.
11. God hath giuen vs an expreſſe
commandement that wee ſhould
not violate the Sabboth daie; and
preſcribed an order how it ſhould
be ſanctified, namelie in holines,
Workes which God requireth on the Sab-both. by calling into minde the ſpiritual
reſt; hearing the worde of G O D,
and ceſſing from worldlie buſines.
Wherevpon *Iſaiah* the Prophet
ſhowing how the ſabboth ſhould
Eſaie. 58, verſe. 13. be obſerued, ſaith, *If thou turne a-*
way thy foote from the Sabboth, from
doing

*doing thy wil on mine holie daie, &
cal the Sabboth a delite, to confecrate
it, as glorious to the Lord, and shalt
honor him, not doing thine owne
waies, nor feeking thine owne wil,
nor speaking a vaine worde, then* Esa.58,14.
*shalt thou delite in the Lord, and I
wil caufe thee to mount vpon the hie
places of the earth, and feede thee
with the heritage of Iaakob thy father: for the mouth of the Lord hath
spoken it.*

Here we fee how the Lord re- *How the*
quireth that this daie fhould be *Sabboth*
obferued; and what reft he looketh *daie is con-*
for at our hands. But, alas, how do *fumed.*
we followe the order which the
Lord hath fet downe! Is not the
Sabboth of al other daies the moft
abufed? which of vs on that daie
is not carried whether his affection leades him vnto al diffolutenes
of life? How often do wee vfe on
that

that daie vnreuerend speeches? which of vs hath his hart occupied in the feare of God? who is not led awaie to the beholding of those spectacles, the sight whereof can bring but confusion both to our bodies and soules?

* At plaies.
Euerie mē-
ber of man
defiled at
plaies.

Are not our eies (there ⋆) carried awaie with the pride of vanitie? our eares abused with amorous, that is lecherous, filthie, and abhominable speech? Is not our tong, which was giuen vs onelie to glorifie God withal, is not our tong there imploied to the blaspheming of Gods holie Name, or the commendation of that is wicked? Are not our hartes through the pleasure of the flesh, the delight of the eie, and the fond motions of the mind, withdrawen from the seruice of the Lord, & meditation of his goodnes?

So

So that albe it is a shame to saie it, yet doubtles whosoeuer wil mark with what multitudes those idle places are replenished, & how emptie the Lordes sanctuarie is of his people, may wel perceaue what deuotion w haue. We maie wel saie, wee are the seruants of the Lord: but the slender seruice wee do him, and the smal regard we haue of his commandements, declares our want of loue towardes him. For, *If yee loue me*, saith Christ, *keepe my commandements.* We maie wel be hirelings, but we are none of his houshold.

Iohn. 14, verse. 15.

Wherfore abuse not so the Sabboth daie, my brethren, leaue not the temple of the Lord; sit not stil in the quagmire of your owne lustes: but put to your strength to helpe your selues, before your owne waight sinke you downe to hel.

Eph.5, 16. hel. *Redeeme the time, for the daies are euil.*

Alas, what folie is in you, to purchaſe with a penie damnation to your ſelues? why ſeeke yee after ſinne, as after a banket? None delight in thoſe ſpectacles, but such as would be made ſpectacles. Account not of their droſſe; their treſures are too baſe to be laied vp in the rich coaſers of your minde. Repentance is furtheſt from you, when you are neareſt ſuch maie-games. Al of you, for the moſt part, do leeſe the time, or rather wilfulie caſt the ſame awaie; contemning that as nothing, which is ſo pretious as your liues cannot redeeme.

None de-light in cō-mun ſpecta-cles, but ſuch as wo uld be ſpectacles.

Time would not be loſt. I would to God you would beſtowe the time you conſume in thoſe vanities in ſeeking after vir-tue, & glorie. For to ſpeake trulie, whatſoeuer

whatſoeuer is not conuerted to the vſe wherefore it was ordained, maie be ſaid to be loſt. For to this end was man borne, and had the benefit of time giuen him, that he might honor, ſerue, and loue his Creator, & thinke vpon his goodnes. For whatſoeuer is done without this is, doubtles caſt awaie.

End of mãs creation.

Oh, how can yee then excuſe your ſelues for the loſſe of time! do ye imagine that your careleſſe life ſhal neuer bee brought into queſtion. Thinke yee the wordes of *S. Paule* the Apoſtle are ſpoken in vaine, when he ſaith, *VVe muſt al appeare before the iudgment ſeate of Chriſt, that euerie man maie receiue the things which are done in his bodie, according to that he hath done, whether it be good or euil.* When that account ſhalbe taken, I feare me your reckoning wilbe to ſeeke.

2.Cor. 5, verſe. 10.

feeke.

But you faie, tufh al is wel, can the Lord fee this? wel, folowe the thoughtes of your owne harts, & fee what fhal come vpon you? yee fhal find al your imaginations to be wicked; and though you flatter your felues in your finnes, tempt the Lord in his mercie, and pricke forward his flownes of wrath by your prefumption : yet he will ftrike in the end to your vtter cõ-

Eccl.7, 19. fufion . *Be thou not wicked ouermuch, neither be thou foolish, wherefore shouldest thou perish not in thy time,* faith Ecclefiaftes godlie. And

Prou. 30, *Salomon, If thou hast bene foolish* verfe. 32. *in lifting vp thy selfe, and if thou hast thought wickedlie, laie thine hande* * Ceffe from *vpon thy mouth.* ★ Again, *Blessed* il doing. *is the man that feareth alwaie, but* Prou. 28, verfe. 14. *he that hardeneth his harte shal fal into euil.*

                  What

What shal I saie? None but the wicked fauor iniquitie. The despisers of G O D, looke where they take anie pleasure, and find sweetnes, there they hold them-selues, and feede their greedie humors; & it falleth out, as Salomon saith, that he who is throughlie an hungred, thinkes the meate which he eateth to be sweete, although it be as bitter as wormewood.

Those vnsauerie morsels of vnseemelie sentences passing out of the mouth of a ruffenlie plaier doth more content the hungrie humors of the rude multitude, and carieth better rellish in their mouthes, than the bread of the worde, which is the foode of the soule.

They are alwaies eating, & neuer satisfied; euer seeing, and neuer contented; continualie hearing, &

neuer wearied; they are greedie of
wickednes, and wil let no time, nor
spare for anie weather (so great is
their deuotion to make their pil-
grimage) to offer their penie to the
Diuel.

The nature   It is the nature of the wicked.
of sinne.   to finde alwaie such sweetenes in
their misdoings, as they wil neuer
giue ouer, til they be ouerthrowen
by Gods righteous iudgement, or
reclamed by the secret working of
his holie spirit.

Caluin vp-   Looke vpon an whore-master,
en Iob,chap. if he be once chased with his owne
74.   lust, the Diuel blindes him, and
makes him take such pleasure in
his wickednes, that al his delight
is therein. If a mã be giuen to drõkennes, or to other wickednes, he
wil hardlie be reclamed, or giue it
ouer, so great sweetenes doth he
tast in those vnseemelie pleasures,
                                        if

if fo I maie faie. Thus you maie
fee the defpifers of God do finde
fweetenes in al their mifdoings.

O my deere brethren, let not
your affections carie you to wickednes; it behooueth you to be
verie warie, and circumfpect how
you thruft your felues into publique affemblies of prophane
plaies, fince there be fo manie inticements vnto loofenes, & fo manie meanes to traine you to vnthriftines there, as wonder it is, if
you haunt them but your foules
wilbe grieuouflie hurt.

Pleafure their capitaine is fo po-
litique an enimie, that he knowes
how to traine you into danger.
But when ye are once within his
lap, hard wil it be for you to ef-
cape. becaufe he can vfe you fo
freendlie, and fo fitlie applie himfelfe to your appetites, that yee wil

rather wiſh to be in bondage with
him, than at libertie without him.
So that yee are warelie to ſhun his
ambuſhes, and ſo to retire, that Satan be not able to endamage you
anie kind of waie. And that you
maie do it the better, it is meete
that yee be made priuie to his ſub-
tile pollicies.

It was trulie ſaid of *Chryſoſtome*,
that none is hurt but of himſelfe;
no man hath ſo dangerous a foe,
as that he caries about him. The
ſnake in our boſome, which wee
nuriſh with ſuch care, wil ſooneſt
annoie vs. Let vs throwe awaie
our fleſhlie minds, and bridle our
affections. For if they maie haue
the hed, they wil neuer leaue running til they haue ouerthrowen
vs, and brought vs to a wretched
ſtate.

In the beginning euerie diſeaſe
is

is to be stopped, and cured; but if a sore run ouer-long it wil growe past the cure of the Physition.

The Magistrate is therefore to prouide in time a remedie to re-dresse the mischiefes that are like to ensue by this common plague. They which gouerne the state are to trie, and decerne each cause, that they appeare not to deale vnadui-sedlie. They are to be diligent to finde out the truth of things; and when a matter is knowen of them to be euil, it is their part to re-forme it; otherwise by negligence they shal run into the displeasure of God. *Dutie of a Magistrate.*

The Magistrates hart must be as the hart of a Lion. He is not to shrinke in the Lordes cause, or to stand in feare to reforme abuses of the Common-weale, because of some particular men of auctoritie. *Virtues of a Magistrate.*

He

He muſt haue both ſtoutnes, and conſtancie to repreſſe euil . And then doubtles the Lord wil bleſſe them in their enterpriſes. Let not therefore the interceſſion of the mightie mooue the Magiſtrate to ſtaie his ſworde from doing iuſtice on the wicked.

The parcialitie which is vſed in theſe daies for fauor, makes theſe yonkers to become bolder by reaſon of thoſe liberties which are granted them. They vphold themſelues by the countenance of their maiſters:as if their auctoritie were a warrant ſufficient for them to do euil,and to beare them out againſt good orders.

Let not the abuſe of the Sabboth proceede further and further, and in the meane while the iudge be a looker on, daring not for feare to reforme their diſorder til al be

out

out of order. Alas, that priuate affection fhould fo raigne in the
Nobilitie, that to pleafure, as they
thinke, their feruants, and to vphold them in their vanitie, they
fhould reftraine the Magiftrates
from executing their office! what
credite can returne to the Noble,
to coūtenance his men to exercife
that qualitie which is not fuffer-
able in anie Cōmon-weale? wher-
as it was an ancient cuftome, that
no man of Honor fhould reteine
anie man, but fuch as was excellent in fome one good qualitie or
other, whereby if occafion fo fer-
ued, he might get his owne liuing?
Then was euerie noble mãs houfe
a Common-weale in it felfe: but
fince the reteining of thefe Cater-
pillers, the credite of Noble men
hath decaied, & they are thought
to be couetous by permitting their
feruants,

A note for Noble-men.

Plaiers
bold beg-
gers.

seruants, which cannot liue of the-
selues, and whome for neerenes
they wil not maintaine, to liue at
the deuotion or almes of other
men, passing from countrie to
countrie, from one Gentlemans
house to another, offering their
seruice, which is a kind of begge-
rie. Who in deede, to speake more
trulie, are become beggers for their
seruants. For comonlie the goodwil men beare to their Lordes,
makes them drawe the stringes of
their purses to extend their liberalitie to them; where otherwise they
would not.

By such infamous persons much
time is lost; and manie daies of honest trauel are turned into vaine
exercises. Wherein is learned nothing but abuse; poore men liuing
on their handie labor, are by them
trained vnto vnthriftines; scholers
by

by their gaudes are allured from
their studies.

Thus the people are robbed;
youth corrupted; the Sabboth prophaned; and of al these euils, who
are counted the vpholders but the
Noble, who of right should establish the lawe of the *Roman Tra-* Traiane
iane, who commanded that no the Empe-
plaier, iester, nor iugler should be ror.
admitted in his Common-weale
to pick the purses of his subiects,
but that they should either learne
some occupation to mainteine
themselues in their owne houses,
or otherwise be banished out of
Rome. But now such like men, vnder the title of their maisters or as
reteiners, are priuiledged to roaue
abroad, and permitted to publish
their mametree in euerie Temple Temples
of God, and that throughout En- prophaned
gland, vnto the horrible contempt with plaies.
of

of praier. So that now the Sanctuarie is become a plaiers ſtage,
and a den of theeues and adulterers.

*Why the
Emp. Tra-
iane ordai-
ned but 22.
holie-daies
throughout
the yeere.*

It was ordained in *Rome* by that
aforeſaid Emperor, that the *Romans* ſhould obſerue but 22. holie daies throughout the whole
yeere. For he thought without al
doubting, that the gods were more
ſerued on ſuch daies as the *Romans* did labor, than on ſuch daies
as they reſted: becauſe the vices
were moe then which they did
commit, than the ſacrifices they
did offer.

And truſt me I am of that opinion, that the Lord is neuer ſo il
ſerued as on the holie-daies. For
then hel breakes loaſe. Then wee
permit our youth to haue their
ſwinge; and when they are out of
the ſight of their maiſters, ſuch
gouern-

gouernment haue they of themfelues, that what by il companie
they meete withal, & il examples
they learne at plaies, I feare me, I
feare me their harts are more alie-
nated in two houres from virtue,
than againe maie wel be amended
in a whole yeare.

But let vs leaue to fpeake here-
of, and returne we to the further
abufe of thefe plaies, which is in
breach of the firft Table of the cō-
mandements . Is it not expreflie
commanded of God in Deutero-
nomie, *That we should not take his* Deu.11,5.
Name in vaine, either by fwearing
rashlie, or falflie? Are we not flatlie
warned , if wee doe infringe the
fame, that he wil not hold vs gilt-
les? yet how wel this commandement is kept at plaies , no man
which refortes to heare them, but
can report.

How

How often is the sacred, and re-uerend Name of God blasphemed on the stages, without regard of his iudgements! Is not he held the gallantest rufler, that can rap out the most disguised othes, to tempt the Lord withal! As who should saie, it were allowable to sweare, so it were done couertlie. As if it were none offence to resemble the wic-ked; and that to dissemble were commendable.

*Matth. 5,
verse. 34.* Christ hath willed vs not to sweare at al , but these felowes thinke they maie iugle with God, as they do with the world. There-fore to verefie their false-hoodes they take the names of *Iupiter, Sa-turne, Iuno,* & such like prophane Gods, as they are called, and God-desses of the Gentils, and that they thinke they maie doe lawfulie. But, if that be not lawful which by the

the Scripture is not warranted, I dare auar that that ſwearing is as odious as the other; and as plainlie forbidden by the worde of God. As we maie read in *Exodus*; where among other things that God ſet-teth downe for the Iſraelits to do, he giueth this vnto them as a prin-cipal charge, that they make no mention of the names of other Gods; that they open not their lips to ſpeake of them; or to ſweare by them, or otherwiſe. And hereupon *Dauid* ſaith, *That the ſorowes of them which offer to another GOD ſhalbe multiplied, their offerings of bloud,* ſaith he, *wil I not offer, nei-ther make mention of their names with my lips.*

Exod. 23, verſe. 13.

Pſal. 16, 4.

How then can theſe men excuſe them-ſelues, that they haue not offered this ſacrifice of bloud! when they not onelie name thoſe

Plaiers o-pen idola-ters.

prophane

prophane gods in their mouthes,
and take them as witnesses of their
falshood, shal wee not saie they
haue consented to idolatrie? I re-
fer their cause to be considered of
the learned, my self maie not passe
beyond my latchet: but this much
I dare affirme, that these men
which dallie with God with their
blasphemous swearings, are not
out of the danger of his indignati-
on, and without repentance shalbe no partakers of Christ, nor of
his merites.

For al their othes what are they
but open reproches against the
Name of God? When these men
sweare, as they sweare at aduen-
ture, doth it not declare that they
regard not the Name of G O D,
which ought to be holden holie in
our sight? *VVho so sweareth vainlie*
Leuit. 19, *by the Name of the Lord, defileth it.*
verse. 12.
The

The Iſraelitiſh womans ſonne for *Leuit. 24,* blaſpheming the Name of the *verſe. 10.* Lord, was ſtoned to death.   *11,&c.*

How is it, my deere brethren, *Who can* that we can heare the Name of the *heare plaies and not ab-* Lord vttered from the mouth of *hor them.* theſe blaſphemers, without ca-ſting downe our heads, and ac-knowleging his infinite maieſtie! How is it that we can heare, with-out ſtopping our eares, ſo manie counterfet othes vttered of plaiers! which, as light as they ſeeme in *Hearers of plaies are acceſſarie* our eies, are great reproches, and *acceſſarie* iniuries to the Maieſtie of GOD. *to the wic-* Wherevnto yee are acceſſarie, in-*kednes of* aſmuch as, yee can vouchſafe to *plaiers.* heare them without ſcruple of có-ſcience. But it appeareth yee haue litle conſcience, and therefore be ſo litle moued.

Others there be which flatter *Defenders* themſelues in euil, accopting that *of plaies.*

pretious

pretious which is most prophane.
They wil stand in contention, and
defend the cause of the wicked,
yea they haue prepared·argumēts
againſt Gods children ; ſo ſmal
power haue they to withſtand the
fancies which the diuel putteth into their heads. Wel, let theſe men
make their arguments, as ſure as
they can , though they haue an
hundred replies in the defence of
the wicked, yea, and ſuch as maie
ſeeme to carie good likelihood for
the maintenance of their cauſe :
yet ſhal they be as nothing, but fal
to the earth, when the iudge of the
cauſe ſhal argue againſt them .
What ſhal I ſaie? wickednes ſo en-
creaſeth , and groweth more and
more to ripenes, when men giue it
ſcope, & ſeeke not to redreſſe it in
A note of conuenient time . When the wic-
Magiſtraſs. ked are ſuffered and not repreſſed,
we

we muſt needs ſaie the Magiſtrate
is a cauſe of ſuch miſbehauior.
Sixe ſcore yeeres before the floud,
the world did ſo exceede in volup-
tuouſnes and pleaſure, as if the
Lord had left to take the charge of
men : but whileſt they liued ſo at
pleaſure & eaſe, their arrainement
was preparing in heauen ; & when
their ſinne was ripe, the Lord pro-
nounced iudgement againſt thoſe
wicked liuers ; rained from heauen, & made a general ſubmerſion
of the whole worlde. I cannot o-
therwiſe think, but that the wrath
of God hanges ouer vs, and that
our arrainment is alredie drawen :
we lacke but our iudgment, which
can pronounce nothing but death
and damnation , the ſinnes of al
men are ſo greeuous.

If we would conſider the ſhort-
nes of our life, which with the tur-
G.j.   ning

ning of an hande maie be cut off, we could not be ſo careles of our ſelues. But the pleaſures of this life ſo beguile vs, & drawe vs from the cōſideration of our eſtate, that we are vtterlie vnmindful of our duties, and forgetful of God, and his worde. But let vs not thinke that God in ſparing vs of his mercie, doth giue libertie for to ſinne; as though we might do wickedlie becauſe we are vnpuniſhed. Oh let vs not delaie our amendment til he ſmite, but rather with the repenting Niniuites aduiſedlie preuent his iudgements : otherwiſe, when we ſhal ſaie like reprobates, 1.Theſſ.5, *Peace, and ſalfetie, then ſhal come* verſe. 3. *vpon vs ſudden deſtruction.*

Alas that we ſhould ſo vnmeaſurablie folowe thoſe vanities, which God condemneth. Thoſe pleaſures of the ſtage, what are they,

they, but the drifts of Satan, which he vseth to blind our eies withal, the more easilie to carie vs from the obedience of GOD! Such knacks from time to time he hath set vp, and men haue willinglie folowed that which they haue liked of, and which the pleasure of the flesh hath drawen them vnto. Yea now adaies we see manie that onlie seeke after those vaine delights, counting no time wel spent, but that they consume in beholding of gaudes.

And albe these pastimes were not (as they are) to be condemned simplie of their owne nature : yet because they are so abused they are abhominable. For the foole no sooner showeth himselfe in his colors to make men merrie, but straight-waie lightlie there foloweth some vanitie, not onlie super-

G.ij.   fluous,

fluous, but beaſtlie and wicked.

Yet are we ſo caried awaie with his vnſeemelie geſture, and vnre-uerend ſcorning, that wee ſeeme onelie to be delighted in him; and are not content to ſport our ſelues with modeſt mirth, as the matter giues occaſion, vnles it be inter-mixed with knauerie, dronken merie-ments, craftie cooſenings, vndecent iuglings, clowniſh con-ceites,& ſuch other curſed mirth, as is both odious in the ſight of God,& offenſiue to honeſt eares, being forbidden by S.Paule in his epiſtle vnto the Epheſians, where he willeth vs expreſlie, that *Nei-*

Epheſ.5,3. *ther filthines, neither fooliſh tal-*
4. *king, nor ieſting, which are things not comelie, ſhould be once named among vs.* Al which things wee now count but light ſinnes (ſo blinde we are, and ſo far paſt our ſelues,

(felues,& the knowledge of God.)

No zelous hart but muſt needs bleed,to ſee how manie Chriſtian ſoules are there ſwalowed vp in the whirle-poole of diuelifh impudencie . Whofoeuer fhal viſit the chappel of Satan, I meane the Theater , fhal finde there no want of yong ruffins, nor lacke of harlots, vtterlie paſt al fhame : who preſſe to the fore-frunt of the ſcaffoldes, to the end to fhowe their impudencie,and to be as an obiect to al mens eies. Yea, ſuch is their open fhameles behauior,as euerie man maie perceaue by their wanton geſtures, wherevnto they are giuen : yea,they ſeeme there to be like brothels of the ſtewes . For often without reſpect of the place, and companie which behold them they commit that filthines openlie,which is horrible to be done in
secret;

Theaters the chappels of Sa-. tan.

The open wickednes of harlots at plaies.

secret; as if whatſoeuer they did,
were warranted. For neither reuerence, iuſtice, nor anie thing beſide
can gouerne them.

An admo-
nition to
Magiſtrats.
Alas, that youth ſhould become
ſo diueliſh, and voide of the feare
of God. Let Magiſtrates aſſure
themſelues, that without ſpeedie
redreſſe al things wil growe ſo far
out of order, as they wilbe paſt remedie. Shamefaſtnes, & modeſtie
is quite baniſhed from yong men:
they are vtterlie ſhameles, ſtub-
borne, and impudent.

It was wel ſaid of Caluine, that
a man ſetled in euil, wil make but
a ſcof of religion. He preacheth in
vaine, that preacheth vnto the
deafe. Tel manie of theſe men of
the Scripture, they wil ſcof, and
turne it vnto a ieſt. Rebuke them
for breaking the Sabboth day, they
wil ſaie, you are a man of the Sabboth,

both, you are verie precife; you wil allowe vs nothing; you wil haue nothing but the worde of God; you wil permit vs no recreation, but haue men like Affes, who neuer reft but when they are eating.

Seeke to withdrawe thefe felowes from the Theater vnto the fermon, they wil faie, By the preacher they maie be edified, but by the plaier both edified and delighted. So that in them the faieng of S. Paule is verified, where he faith, that *The wifedome of the flesh is nothing, but enimitie againft G O D.* Rom. 8, 7. How fmal heede take they of thefelues, which fuffer their owne wicked affections to withdrawe them from God, and his worde. We neede not voluntarilie feeke our owne deftruction. For he that is virtuouflie difpofed, fhal finde lewde perfons enough to withdrawe

drawe him from wel doing by the promise of pleasure, and delightful pastime, wherevnto we are naturalie inclined, vnto the Schoolehouse of Satan, and chappel of il counsel, where he shal see so much iniquitie, & loasenes; and so great outrage and scope of sinne, that it is a wonder, if he returne not either wounded in conscience, or changed in life.

Theaters the schoole-house of Satan, and chappels of il counsel.

I would wish therefore al maisters, not onlie to withdraw themselues, but their seruants also frō such wicked assemblies. For it is alwaies wisedome to shun the occasions of euil.

Counsel to maisters.

Youth wilbe withdrawen by companie, if they be not restrained of their libertie. They neede not to seeke out for schoole-masters, they can learne euil too fast of them-selues, and are pregnant
enough

enough at home to learne vnhap-
pines. Manie of nature honeſt, and
tractable , haue bene altered by
thoſe ſhowes and ſpectacles, and
become monſterous. Mans minde,
which of it ſelfe is proane vnto
vice, is not to be pricked forward
vnto wantonnes, but bridled : if it
be left vnto it ſelfe, it hardlie ſtandeth ; if it be driuen forth, it run-
neth headlong.

Flee far from Babylon, yee that
carrie the Lordes veſſels . Forſo- Rom. 6, 3.
much as yee are baptized into
Chriſt, it ſtandeth you vpõ to be
holie both of bodie and minde, &
to dedicate your ſelues to his ſeruice, which yee ſhal neuer do, vnles ye withdraw your ſelues from
the inticements of vanitie, and eſ-
chue the occaſions of euil, which
that yee maie the better do, yee are
to faſten your eies vpon God, by
                                    whome

whome we are sanctified.

*Il examples
to be shun-
ned.*

Let not the examples of the wicked be a president vnto vs; neither
let vs be drawen away to euil with
the multitude. Custome shal but
make vs bold in sin, and the companie of scorners make vs more
impudent, and disordered of life.

It is not enough for vs to excuse our selues by the doings of o-
ther men; it wil not be taken for an
excuse, although we could alleage
that euerie man doth as wee doe.
For it is no meanes to acquite vs
before God, to saie that other be
no better than our selues. I would
rather wish that the euil conuersa-
tion of others might be an occasion to drawe vs backe; least perhaps
we be wrapped in the vices that
raigne in al the wicked, and so be
partakers of the punishment due
to them. For we are not to walke

as

as men that looke but onlie vpon the creatures, but our part is to set God before our eies, whose presence we cannot possiblie escape.

It is maruelous to consider how *Motion of* the gesturing of a plaier, which *the bodie.* *Tullie* termeth the eloquence of the bodie, is of force to moue, and prepare a man to that which is il. For such thinges be disclosed to the eie, and to the eare, as might a great deale better be kept close. Whereby a double offence is committed; first by those dissolute plaiers, which without regard of honestie, are not ashamed to exhibite the filthiest matters they can deuise to the sight of men: secondly by the beholders, which vouchsalfe to heare and behold such filthie things, to the great losse both of themselues and the time. There cometh much euil in at the eares, but

but more at the eies, by theſe two open windowes death breaketh into the ſoule. Nothing entereth in more effectualie into the memorie, than that which commeth by ſeeing; things heard do lightlie paſſe awaie, but the tokens of that which wee haue ſeene, ſaith *Petrarch*, ſticke faſt in vs whether we wil or no : and yet they enter not into vs, vnles we be willing, except verie ſeldome.

Alack what violence carieth vs awaie, to be merie an hower, and alwaies after to be ſad; to ſee that at one time, which a thouſande times after wee ſhal rue that euer we ſawe it !

Manie haue ben intangled with the webs of theſe Spiders, who would gladlie haue bene at libertie when they could not . The webs are ſo ſubtillie ſpun, that
there

there is no man that is once within them, that can auoide them
without danger. None can come
within those snares that maie escape vntaken, be she maide, ma-
trone, or whatsoeuer; such force
haue their inchantements of pleasure to drawe the affections of the
mind.

Snares of plaies.

This inward fight hath vanqui-
shed the chastitie of manie women; some by taking pittie on the
deceitful teares of the stage louers,
haue bene mooued by their complaint to rue on their secret frends,
whome they haue thought to
haue tasted like torment; some hauing noted the ensamples how
maidens restrained from the mar-
riage of those whome their frends
haue misliked, haue there learned
a policie to preuent their parents,
by stealing them awaie; some seeing

ing by enfample of the ftage plaier
one carried with too much liking
of an other mans wife, hauing noted by what practife fhe hath bene
affailed and ouertaken, haue not
failed to put the like in effect in
earneft, that was afore fhowen in
ieft.

The wilines & craft of the ftage
is not yet fo great, as is without
on the fcaffoldes. For that they
which are euil difpofed, no fooner
heare anie thing fpoken that maie
ferue their turne, but they applie it
vnto themfelues. Alas, faie they to
their familiar by them, Gentle-
woman, is it not pittie this pafsio-
ned louer fhould be fo martyred.
And if he finde her inclining to
foolifh pittie, as commonlie fuch
women are, then he applies the
matter to himfelfe, and faies that
he is likewife caried awaie with
                              the

the liking of her; crauing that pittie to be extended vpõ him, as she seemed to showe toward the afflicted amorous stager.

These running headed louers are growen so perfect scholers by long continuance at this schoole, that there is almost no worde spoken, but they can make matter of it to serue their turne. They can so surelie discouer the conceits of the minde, and so cunninglie handle themselues; & are growen so subtile in working their matters, that neither the ielosie of *Iuno,* who suspecteth al things; nor the streight keeping of *Danaes* maie debar; nor the watchfulnes of *Argoes* with his hundred eies espie.

Credite me, there can be found out no stronger engine to batter the honestie as wel of wedded wiues, as the chastitie of vnmarried

Flie Theaters you that would be honest.

ried

ried maides and widowes, than are
the hearing of common plaies.
There wanton wiues fables, and
paſtorical ſonges of loue, which
they vſe in their comical diſcour-
ſes (al which are taken out of the
ſecret armorie of *Venus*, & practiſing bawderie) turne al chaſtitie
vpſide downe, & corrupt the good
diſpoſition & manners of youth,
inſomuch that it is a miracle, if
there be foūd anie either woman,
or maide, which with theſe ſpectacles of ſtrange luſt, is not often-
times inflamed euen vnto furie.

The nature of their Comedies
are, for the moſt part, after one
manner of nature, like the tragical
Comedie of *Caliſtus*; where the
bawdreſſe *Sceleſtina* inflamed the
maiden *Melibœia* with her ſorce-
ries. Do wee not vſe in theſe diſ-
courſes to counterfet witchcraft,
charmed

charmed drinkes, & amorous po-
tions, thereby to drawe the affections of men, & to stir them vp vnto lust, to like euen those whome
of them-selues they abhor . The
ensamples whereof stirre vp the
ignorant multitude to seeke by
such vnlawful meanes the loue, &
goodwil of others.

I can tel you a storie of like *A strange*
practise vsed of late by a ielous *example.*
wife to her husband, whose hart
being, as she thought, estranged o-
therwise than of custome, did practise with a sorceresse to haue some
powder, which might haue force
to renew her husbandes wonted
goodwil towardes her: but it had
such a virtue in the operation, as it
wel nigh brought him his bane:
for his memorie therby was gone:
so that if God had not dealt mira-
culouslie with him, by reuealing
H.j. it,

it, it had cost him his life. The like
we read of *Lucullus* and *Lucretius*,
who by drinking such amorous
confections lost first their wits, &
afterward their liues.

The deuise of carrieng and re-
carrieng letters by landresses, pra-
ctising with pedlers to transport
their tokens by colorable meanes,
to sel their marchandise, and other
kind of policies to beguile fathers
of their children, husbands of their
wiues, gardens of their wardes,
He mea- and maisters of their seruants,
neth plaies, is it not aptlie taught in the
who are not
vnfitlie so Schoole of abuse *: But hush no
called. more.

I am sorie this schoole is not
pluckt downe by the Magistrate;
and the schoole-masters banished
London. this citie. ★ Thus much I wil tel
them, if they suffer these brothel
houses to continue, or do in anie
wise

wife allowe them, the Lord wil
faie vnto them, as the Pfalmiſt
faith, *If thou ſaweſt a theefe thou
wenteſt with him, and haddeſt thy
part with adulterers; thou haſt done
theſe things, and becauſe I haue held
my peace,thou haſt beleeued,wicked
man,that I am like vnto thee,but I
wil accuſe thee,&c.*

The reuerend word of God , &
hiſtories of the Bible ſet forth on
the ſtage by theſe blaſphemous
plaiers,are ſo corrupted with their
geſtures of ſcurrilitie,and ſo interlaced with vncleane, and whoriſh
ſpeeches,that it is not poſsible to
drawe anie profite out of the do-
ctrine of their ſpiritual morali-
ties. For that they exhibite vnder
laughing that which ought to be
taught and receiued reuerendlie.
So that their auditorie maie returne madde merie in minde, but
none

none comes awaie reformed in manners. And of al abuſes this is moſt vndecent and intollerable, to ſuffer holie things to be handled by men ſo prophane, and defiled by interpoſitiō of diſſolute words.

Againſt Auctors of plaies.

The writers of our time are ſo led awaie with vaineglorie, that their onlie endeuor is to pleaſure the humor of men; & rather with vanitie to content their mindes, than to profit them with good enſample. The notableſt lier is become the beſt Poet; he that can make the moſt notorious lie, and diſguiſe falſhood in ſuch ſort, that he maie paſſe vnperceaued, is held the beſt writer. For the ſtrangeſt Comedie brings greateſt. delectation, and pleaſure. Our nature is led awaie with vanitie, which the auctor perceauing frames himſelf with nouelties and ſtrange trifles

to

to content the vaine humors of
his rude auditors, faining countries neuer heard of, monsters and
prodigious creatures that are not:
as of the Arimaspie, of the Grips,
the Pigmeies, the Cranes, & other
such notorious lies. And if they
write of histories that are knowen,
as the life of *Pompeie*; the martial
affaires of *Cæsar,* and other wor-
thies, they giue them a newe face,
and turne them out like counter-
feites to showe themselues on the
stage. It was therefore aptlie applied of him, who likened the writers of our daies vnto Tailors, who
hauing their sheers in their hand,
can alter the facion of anie thing
into another forme, & with a new
face make that seeme new which
is old. The shreds of whose curio-
sitie our Historians haue now sto-
len from them, being by practise
become

Writers of
these daies.

become as cunning as the Tailor to set a new vpper-bodie to an old coate; and a patch of their owne to a peece of anothers.

The best thing at plaies is starke naught.

So that yee shal find in al their writings three differences, manie things good, manie things indifferent, and manie starke naught: but by reason that thing which is good is applied vnto il purpose, & mixed with euil, the good hath changed propertie, and is become of the nature of the bad. Otherwise goodnes & badnes, being two côtraries, cannot be made to agree together. And therefore there can be no difference of choice, but al must be euil: because it is generallie il applied, and by altering propertie, hath changed his nature. Yet neuertheles that it keepeth his virtue, of being good, and reduced to his proper substance.

I

I do not denie, but that writers
in al their workes maie be plea-
fant, fo far forth as they be profitable, and fwarue not from hone-
ftie, and therein deferue commendation. But what praife maie they
deferue who fet forth thofe works
which are vaine and naught, and
conteine in them no matter of
good example, who write of thofe
things, which may corrupt the life
of men , thereby making them
worfe by ten to one, than they
were before they heard them?

What doe they leaue behind
them ? monumentes of wanton
wicked life, and doting things for
men of thefe latter daies. O Lord,
how do thofe wanton wordes of
theirs intice vnto wicked life, and
with a poifoned baite allure men
to finne! Their wanton fpeeches
do pearfe our fecret thoughts, and
moue

moue vs thereby vnto mischiefe,
and prouoke our members to vncleannes.

*An Obie-
ction.*

But some perhaps wil saie, The
Noble man delighteth in such
things, whose humors must be
contented, partlie for feare, & partlie for commoditie : and if they
write matters pleasant, they are
best preferred in court-among the
cunning heads.

Cunning heads, whose wits are
neuer wel exercised, but in the pra-
Answere. ctise of such exploits! But are those
things to be suffered and praised,
because they please the rich, and
content the Noble man, that alwaies liues in ease? not so. A two
legged Asse maie be clothed in
gold, a man of honor maie be corrupt of iudgement, though by his
auctoritie he maie seeme wiser
than *Socrates,* whome *Phœbus* for
wisedome

wifedome iudged to beare the bel.
Thofe goodlie perfons, if they be
voide of virtue, maie wel be counted like faire clothes ouer a foule
wal; big bladers ful of wind, yet of
no waight. Where wealth is abun-
dant, pleafure is prefent : pleafure
bringeth folie into eftimation; and
thereby the light of reafon is vtterlie extinguifhed.

Who writeth for reward, neither regardeth virtue, nor truth ;
but runs vnto falfhood, becaufe he
flattereth for commoditie. Neede
and flatterie are two brothers, and
the eldeft feruitors in the Court:
they were both fcholers vnto *Ariftippus*, and learned both of them
to applie themfelues to the time,
& their matter to the difpofition?
No maruel then though none can
pleafe *Dionyfius* but *Ariftippus*, nor
anie the courtier but the flatterer.

Writers for reward.

The

The rich that followeth the plea-ſures of this life, maie not abide to be reformed, or to be drawen away from his deſires, be they neuer ſo wicked and vnſeemelie. Talke to him of amendement, he wil ſaie, he is not dieng. He that repre-hends him, is a Preacher; he that ſooths him, is a Saint. Who med-dels with nettles cannot paſſe vn-ſtinged: and he that deales with men of auctoritie otherwiſe than maie like them, cannot ſcape from his danger without hurt. I maie not ſtaie longer on this point.

As I haue had a ſaieng to theſe verſi-fieng Plaie-makers: ſo muſt I likewiſe deale with ſhameles in-actors. When I ſee by them yong boies, inclining of themſelues vn-to wickednes, trained vp in filthie ſpeeches, vnnatural and vnſeeme-lie geſtures, to be brought vp by theſe

thefe Schoole-mafters in bawde-
rie, and in idlenes, I cannot chufe
bnt with teares and griefe of hart
lament.

O with what delight can the fa- *Plaiers, the*
ther behold his fonne bereft of *fchoolemai-*
fhamefaftnes, & trained vp to im- *fters of fin,*
pudencie! How proane are they *fchoole of*
of themfelues, and apt to receiue *abufe.*
inftruction of their lewde teach-
ers, which are the Schoolemafters
of finne in the fchoole of abufe!
what do they teach them, I praie
you but to fofter mifchiefe in their
youth, that it maie alwaies abide
in them, and in their age bring
them fooner vnto hel?

And as for thofe ftagers them- *Difpofition*
felues, are they not commonlie *of plaiers*
for the moft
fuch kind of men in their conuer- *part.*
fation, as they are in profefsion?
Are they not as variable in hart, as
they are in their partes? are they
not

Plaiers can not better be compared than to the Camelion.

not as good practisers of Bawde-rie,as inactors? Liue they not in such sort themselues, as they giue precepts vnto others ? doth not their talke on the stage declare the nature of their disposition ? doth not euerie one take that part which is proper to his kind? doth not the Plough-mans tong walke of his plough; the Sea-faring man of his mast, cable, and saile; the Soldier of his harnes,speare,and shield; & bawdie mates of bawdie matters ? Aske them, if in their laieng out of their partes, they choose not those partes which is most agree-ing to their inclination, and that they can best discharge? And looke what euerie of them doth most delight in, that he can best handle to the contentment of others. If it be a roisting, bawdie, and lasciui-ous part, wherein are vnseemelie
speeches,

speeches,& that they make choife
of them as beft anfwering, & proper to their manner of plaie: maie
we not faie, by how much he ex-
ceedes in his gefture, he delightes
himfelfe in his part?& by fo much
it is pleafing to his difpofition and
nature? If (it be his nature)to be a
bawdie plaier, and he delight in
fuch filthie & curfed actions, fhal
we not thinke him in his life to be
more difordered, and to abhor
virtue?

But they perhaps wil faie, that *An Obie-*
fuch abufes as are handled on the *ction.*
ftage, others by their examples,
are warned to beware of fuch e-
uils,to amendment.

In deed if their auctoritie were *Anfwere.*
greater than the wordes of the
Scripture; or their zeale of more
force than of the preacher,I might
eafilie be perfuaded to thinke, that
men

men by them might be called vnto
good life. But when I see the word
of truth proceeding from the hart,
and vttered by the mouth of the
reuerend preachers, to be receaued
of the most part into the eare, and
but of a fewe rooted in the hart: I
cannot by anie means beleeue that
the wordes proceeding from a prophane plaier, and vttered in scor-
ning sort, interlaced with filthie,
lewde, & vngodlie speeches, haue
greater force to mooue men vnto
virtue, than the wordes of truth
vttered by the godlie Preacher,
Exo.32,32　whose zeale is such as that of Mo-
ses, who was contented to be ra-
Rom.9, 3.　ced out of the booke of life; and of
Paule, who wished to be separated
from Christ for the welfare of his
brethren. If the good life of a man
be a better instruction to repentace than the tong, or words, why
　　　　　　　　　　do

do not plaiers, I befeech you, leaue examples of goodnes to their po-
fteritie? But which of them is fo zealous, or fo tendereth his owne
faluatiõ, that he doth amend him-felfe in thofe pointes, which, as
they faie, others fhould take heede of? Are they not notoriouflie
knowen to be thofe men in their life abroade, as they are on the
ftage, roifters, brallers, il-dealers, bofters, louers, loiterers, ruffins?
So that they are alwaies exercifed in plaieng their parts; and practi-
fing wickednes; making that an art, to the end they might the better gefture it in their partes. For who can better plaic the ruffin thã
a verie ruffin? who better the lo-uer, than they who make it a com-
mon exercife? To conclude, the *Chiefe end* principal end of all their inter- *of plaies.*
ludes is to feede the world with

fights,

sights, & fond pastimes; to iuggle in good earnest the monie out of other mens purses into their owne hands.

Plaiers in-
famous per-
sons.
Plaiers ba-
nished out
of Rome.

What shal I saie ? They are infamous men; and in *Rome* were thought worthie to be expelled, albe there was libertie enough to take pleasure.

In the pri-
matiue
Church
plaiers
kept from
the Com-
munion.

In the primatiue Church they were kept out from the Communion of Christians, and neuer remitted til they had perfourmed publike penance. And thervpon S. *Cyprian* in a certaine Epistle counseleth a Bishop, not to receiue a plaier into the pension of the Church, by which they were norished, til there was an expresse act of penance with protestation to renounce an art so infamous. And thus much for those plaiers.

Obiection.

Some haue obiected, that by these

thefe publique plaies manie for-
beate to do euil for feare to be
publiquelie reprehended . And
for that caufe they wil faie it
was tolerated in *Rome*, wherein
Emperors were touched, though
they were prefent.

But to fuch it maie be anfwe- *Anfweris*
red, firft that in difguifed plaiers
giuen ouer to al fortes of diffolutenes, is not found fo much as
a wil to do good, feing they care
for nothing leffe than for virtue.
Secondlie, that is not a good
meanes to correct finne. For that
if it be fecret, it ought not to be
reuealed openlie, but by fuch
meanes to be reformed as Chrift
himfelfe alloweth in his Gofpel.
If, faith he, *thy brother trefpaffe* Matth.18,
againft thee, fpeaking of thofe verfe. 15.
fecret & particular finnes, which
are not open, and made knowen

I.j.   to

A 3. blast of retrait
to others, go and tel him his fault
betweene thee and him alone; if
he heare thee, thou hast wonne thy
Matth. 18, *brother. But if he heare thee not,*
verse. 16. *take yet with thee one or two, that*
by the mouth of two or three wit-
nesses euerie worde maie be con-
17. *firmed. And if he wil not vouch-*
safe to heare them, tel it vnto the
Church: (which is, to those ancient & expert men of the Iewes
which were appointed to reforme manners, and execute dif-
cipline. For those affemblies of
ancient Fathers did reprefent the
Church; becaufe they had the
charge thereof appointed vnto
them) *and if he refufe to heare the*
Church alfo, let him be vnto thee
as an Heathen man, and a Pub-
licane.

You fee then that euerie fault
being priuatelie knowen is to be
kept

kept secret, and not to be openlie
vttered to the defamation of the
offender. And that on the other-
side, if it be a matter openlie
knowen, it is to be put to the re-
prehension of the Magiftrate,
and not of the plaier, whofe reprehenfion is as vnreuerend, and
odious, as the reprehenfion of a
Magiftrate is decent, and commendable.

The antiquitie of plaieng is
likewife often vfed for an argu-
ment to proue it allowable. But
the cuftome of euil is not to be
maintained, becaufe of antiquitie. Gods truth is not to be oppreffed vnder that color, what
examples of antiquitie foeuer do
ferue to maintaine wickednes, I
am not bounde to allowe of
them, or to maintaine them. For
my part I difallowe al thofe an-

*An obiecti-
on anfwe-
red.*

*Againft the
antiquitie
of plaies.*

tiquities which are contrarie to the Scriptures. Those spectacles were vsed of the Gentils to the setting vp of idolatrie, and to the honor of their false gods : as *Pesa* and *Elis.* Such games were exercised in the honor of *Iupiter* worshipped on the hil *Olympus*. *Theseus* ordained in the straightes of *Corinth* the *Isthemian* games in the honor of *Neptune*. There were also *Pythij ludi*, *Ludi funebres*, *Lupercalia*, *Saturnalia*, and *Circenses ludi*, and manie other deuised as wel by *Romans* as *Greekes* to the great charges of their Cōmon-weales. The exercise whereof was both bloudie and beastlie, and yet among them sufferable and allowed.

Notwithstanding, these are not examples vnto Christians to allowe

allowe that for good, which was sufferable among them . For then one might slaie another; one might wound another, then should we encounter with wild beastes; our hartes should then delight in shedding bloud; and be al giltie of the death of the murdered.

As for the plaiers in these daies which exhibite their games for lucre sake, as did those two Romans *Esopus*, and *Arossius*, who showed their wonderful cunning on the stage to gather welth and substance; they are of the most part of men either of auctoritie, or learning held for vagabondes, & infamous persons; they maie aptlie be likened vnto droanes, which wil not labor to bring in, but liue of the labors of the painefull gatherers. They

The accopt which good men haue of our cōmon gamesters, and plaiers.

are

are therefore to be thrust out of
the Bee-hiue of a Christian
Common-weale.

This vnhonest trade of gaine,
hath driuen manie from their
occupations, in hope of easier
thrift. What successe they haue
had, some of them haue repor-
ted, finding the Prouerbe true,
that, *Il gotten goodes are il spent*.

Would to God London would followe the example of Marsiles.

The citie *Marsiles*, as *Vale-
rian* writeth, kept so great graui-
tie, that it would receaue into it
no stage-plaiers : because their
arguments, for the most parte,
contained the actes and doinges
of harlots; to the end that the custome of beholding such things
might not also cause a licence of

*Harke Ma-
gistrates of
London.*

folowing them. I would to God
the Magistrates of our citie of
London would haue the like
foresight . The permission of
plaies

plaies fo long a time hath already corrupted this citie ; and brought the Name of the citizens into flander : the examples of Gods iudgement is at this prefent an example in this citie. The finne of whoredome being winked at by the children of *Beniamin*, they were punifhed by the deftructio of their whole tribe . If we flacke to punifh offenders, and giue our felues to maintaine the wicked in their lewdenes , wee are to looke for none other than a general confufion . For the Lord himfelfe wil take part againft the wicked to deftroie them. They maie be wel let alone for a time, but yet that which is deferred wil one daie come.

London defamed thoroughplaies there vfed.

Iudges.19, verfe. 1. 2,&c.

In the raigne of *Tiberius* the Emperor, the Lorde by ouerthrowing

A 3.blast of retrait

A worthie example of Gods iustice vpon a play house, or Theater.
throwing the Amphitheater in the citie of *Tidena* slew 20.thousand of the beholders. A notable example of Gods iustice. For notable offenders he appointeth strange & notable punishments:

Wisd. 11, verse. 13.
And looke wherewith a man sinneth, by the same also shal he be punished.

The conclusion.
Wherfore, my deere brethren, leaue these *Cretan* liers with their wicked inuentions: *Do not* Prou.24,1 Rom.12,2. *companie with the wicked; facion not your selues like vnto this world; but be ye changed by the renuing of your mind, that ye maie proue what is the good wil of God, and acceptable, and perfect; eschew* Psa.34,14. I.Pet.3,11 Prou. 24. verse. 24. 20. *euil and do good . He that shal saie to the wicked, Thou art righteuous, him shal the people cursse, and the multitude shal abhor him. For the Lord is far from the wicked;*
their

their houſe ſhalbe deſtroied, there ſhalbe none end of their plagues, their light ſhalbe put out. Yeelde not your ſelues to them, leſt ye periſh in their wickednes; yeeld not your ſelues to thoſe vaine pleaſures and delights. For yee ſhal find nothing more hurtful, nor preiudicial to your ſoules; they depriue you of al good cogitations; enimies they are vnto virtue; increaſers of wickednes; the nurſes of al vice; the corrupters of manners; the ſubuerters of religion; and ſo bring at the end vnto euerlaſting ſorowes and gnaſhing of teeth in the pit of hel.

The Lord of his infinite mercie looke vpon vs, and direct vs with his holie ſpirit; and ſo order our liues, that wee maie be holie and acceptable in his ſight.

The

The Lord open our eies, that we maie see our sinne, and loath it in our selues, represse it in the wicked, and condemne it in our Common-weale. Lord increase our deuotion, that our hartes maie be made zelous to heare the word of God, *which is a lanterne vnto our feete, and a light vnto our pathes.*

Preserue this Church of England; increase thy flocke vniuersal; be a safegard vnto vs against the force of our enimies, for our trust is in thee.

Blesse our worthie Princesse,& renowmed soueraigne Queene *ELIZABETH,*and establish her state, as the seate of *Dauid*; let thy spirit direct her doings in al things; that she maie be as the zelous *Iosias* to vphold the state of the true Church; to roote

out

out superstition and idolatrie;
that she maie be as a continual
enimie to the enimies of thy
truth. Be thou, ô Lord, her sup-
porter, that thou by her maist
defend thine owne cause.

Merciful God, inspire her ho-
norable Counsel with the wisedome of *Salomon*, that their
counsel maie be wise and good;
and their harts linked vnsepara-
blie together to the preseruation
of her state, and the welfare of
this land.

Lord strengthen the hand of
Iustice against the wicked, that
our Magistrates maie roote out
the memorial of wickednes from
the earth, that our Realme maie
florish,& our liues be as a lampe
on a mountaine, to giue light
vnto other nations how to direct their liues after our good
ex-

example.

Performe al wantes, O God, in thy Church ; increaſe our faith and loue towards thee; continue t'ıy Goſpel among vs for thy deere Sonnes ſake Ieſus Chriſt,to whome with thee,and the holie Ghoſt,be al honor and glorie, worlde without ende, **Amen.**

Epheſ.5, 13.

Al things, when they are reprooued of the light,are manifeſt . For it is light that maketh al things manifeſt.

1580,

¶ Imprinted at London by Henrie
Denham, dwelling in Pater noster
Row, at the figne of the Starre, being
the affigne of William Seres.

Cum priuilegio Regiæ Maieftatis.

FE

BISHOP'S UNIVERSITY
LIBRARY
LENNOXVILLE